Elizabeth Muir-Lewis has two published books. This book, *When the Last Note Sounds,* is a biography about her life as the wife of one of Britain's finest singers, Richard Lewis CBE. As a singer herself she has the unique position of understanding the extraordinary world of the international singer.

Through Richard she heard about that great era after the second world war when British music had a renaissance.

It is a tale of great composers, conductors and singers. Elizabeth brings to life the strenuous world of international singing, its downsides as well as its glories. She does not mince her words but illuminates the art of singing as she saw it.

Elizabeth Muir-Lewis

WHEN THE LAST
NOTE SOUNDS

AUSTIN MACAULEY PUBLISHERS™

LONDON · CAMBRIDGE · NEW YORK · SHARJAH

A CIP catalogue record for this title is available from the British Library.

ISBN 9781398429413 (Paperback)
ISBN 9781398429420 (Hardback)
ISBN 9781398429437 (ePub e-book)

www.austinmacauley.com

First Published 2022
Austin Macauley Publishers Ltd®
1 Canada Square
Canary Wharf
London
E14 5AA

My late husband, Terence Pridmore, who encouraged me and Sir Philip Anson – who was a huge help in reviewing the book for me.

Thanks must also be given to the Richard Lewis Trust for its financial support in publishing this book.

Foreword

Richard Lewis was a giant of post-War music, steeped in the profession from singing the boy in Mendelssohn's Elijah with Isobel Baillie to a glittering career traversing most of the major new operatic and oratorio work of the 1950s and 60s. His contribution, as one of a Pantheon of great singers from that golden era, was central in putting British music on an international footing.

Lewis's widow, Elizabeth, offers us a tribute to Lewis of great charm, always unpretentious, honest, fun and above all with a wonderfully flowing and direct narrative. She paints observant and precise pictures of events, places and people, and there are many of them. The way giants like Beniamino Gigli, Richard Tauber (Lewis took his first name from Tauber and surname from his mother – his birth name, Thomas Thomas, being considered unmanageable) and Kirsten Flagstad appear in the story is touchingly portrayed. The description of Glyndebourne is pure Osbert Lancaster in words. She makes no bones about Richard's glories but she also speaks of the occasional mishaps, in the increasing international arenas in which he performed. Everything is refreshingly believable.

Of course, Lewis's burnished and flexible rendering of Gerontius – as the 'third' and most equipped in the trinity after Gervaise Elwes and Heddle Nash – under Barbirolli (and Sargent before that) – remains the standout artistic achievement as far as the public are concerned. Yet the range of his accomplishments are still vastly under-appreciated. Lewis was a celebrated Classical and Romantic singer in all the major houses, but also a brave exponent of new music. An admiring exponent of Britten's music and gifts (if finding the atmosphere around the composer trying), he was a pioneering voice for Walton, Tippett and was noted for superb performances for Stravinsky and Bernstein. Such was his vocal longevity, certainly for the stresses and strains of his voice type, that he even performed with the likes of Pavarotti and his generation. He was arguably the first 'modern' British tenor.

Elizabeth's down-to-earth memories of life with Richard are always modestly expressed and therefore especially real and engaging for the reader. She rightly reserves her highest praise for Lewis's distinctive amalgam of qualities. In describing how different Richard's Gerontius was from others, she says it plainly and with as much objectivity as any widow can: 'Many tenors have sung it. But Richard Lewis had a special quality that would mark him out as the finest of his generation. He had the power, depth of range as well as a thrilling top. He could spin an exquisite line in pianissimo with magical beauty'.

Chapter One
"When the Last Note Sounds"
Or "The Travelling Troubadour"
The Boy

It was a murky morning, fog lying like a heavy blanket as street lamps glowed hazily through the dampness in the silence of a dead world.

Footsteps passed. Was someone there? Or were they disembodied ghosts, treading cautiously, peering ahead to make sure there was no wall to bump into or collide with another lost soul on such a morning?

A voice called, "Hurry up, Thomas, we'll be late."

A door opened. Number Ten Baden Street.

"I'm coming, Ma," answered a boy's voice.

"Now keep that scarf over your nose, Thomas."

A woman came out, followed by the boy.

"There won't be any buses today, Thomas," said the woman. "We must hurry if we are to get there in time."

Her voice had a lovely Welsh lilt to it. The boy had the Mancunian sound, that harsh northern accent, something he would never lose entirely.

The fog was so dense they had to walk hand in hand in case they lost each other—thick, yellow, dirty, invading everything. Noses. Down collars. Insidious. Stupefying.

The mother shivered, wondering why it had to be like that.

The boy wasn't bothered. He had something to do. He had to sing today.

Finally, they reached the hall. Outside the poster said: 'Festival competition'.

"Here we are, Thomas. Now hurry in, dear; make sure you have your entry ticket."

"Yes Ma… here it is."

He went into the competitors' room. His mother went into the main hall to listen. She was used to this. Every year Thomas entered the competition. In his bedroom, he had a bag of medals. Today though was different. The adjudicator was the great Sir Thomas Armstrong.

"That's right, dear. Sit at the front and wait to be called," whispered the official.

Sir Thomas had been adjudicating since ten o'clock. The competitors had not been bad, but nothing outstanding. He liked to hear children, to encourage them. But after three hours, he longed for a nice cup of tea.

"Number twenty," the official called out.

Thomas gave Sir Thomas the music and stepped up onto the platform. Sir Thomas looked at it: *Panis Angelicus* He groaned to himself. This was the seventh he had heard this morning.

"Off you go, young man," he called.

Thomas took a deep breath, looked over at the pianist, giving a little nod. He was ready. The introduction reached his entry. He started.

Sir Thomas was not expecting very much. This was just a skinny little boy in what was probably his Sunday best. He did have a confident look about him though. In a moment, everything changed. Sir Thomas was jolted out of his lethargy. Out of this boy, barely ten years old, came a true soprano with shimmering tonal quality. And what was most marked, his obvious love of singing.

My God, the boy has it, thought Sir Thomas.

The song ended. A silence fell. People in the audience refrained from clapping just for a second or two. They knew what they had heard, even if not quite sure what.

Sir Thomas now had to mark the singers.

No contest here, he thought, *but I must be fair.*

Thomas came first. No surprise. He always did. But today was different. He had sung to a top man. Maybe he would get a proper opinion.

The competition was over. That was the last class until after lunch. Sir Thomas looked around to see who the boy was with.

"Ah, you are Thomas's mother?"

"Yes, Sir Thomas. Thank you for giving him the first place."

"There was never any doubt, Mrs Thomas. And I wish to tell you that your son is a natural singer. He must be trained, you know."

It would be good to tell you that fifteen years later, Sir Thomas would remember, know what had happened to this little boy. But he would be long gone.

"Well, Thomas," his mother said as they came out into the street back into the fog, now even thicker, "your pa will be pleased, son."

"Yes Ma…Sir Thomas was really nice, wasn't he?"

"He was… and set me a question. He thought you should have singing lessons."

He had indeed set a question. Singing lessons? When they just managed to survive!

"I'll find a way," decided Mrs Thomas.

Chesterton Wesleyan Church.

SUNDAY, NOV. 24th.

TOM THOMAS

THE WONDERFUL BOY SINGER (From Ardwick, Manchester)

Winner Congleton Musical Festival with 92 marks.

Preacher : **Mr. S. JONES,** Alsagers Bank.

Dr. Caradog Roberts says :—
"Tom Thomas is an artiste."

Madam Edith Hands, F.R.A.M., says :—
"He is a born singer."

The "Evening Sentinel" says :—
"He has a rich resonant musical voice."

The "Daily Dispatch" says :—
"Artistic ; a splendid rendering."

AFTERNOON MUSICAL SERVICE AT 2-50.

Chairman : Mr. THOMAS LOVATT
OF HARRISEAHEAD.

EVENING SERVICE AT 6.

Anthems by the Choir.

Conductor : Mr. T. DAVIES.   Organist : Mr. W. A. YATES, L.T.C.L.

COLLECTIONS FOR TRUST FUNDS.

Silver will be thankfully received on entering Gallery in the evening.

Chapter Two

And a way was found. Thomas's father sang in a local choir. The choir master was a Mr Evans. Soon Thomas was going every week to Mr Evans for lessons. It didn't take his teacher long to know that here was an exceptional pupil, a boy avid for knowledge.

"Like a sponge he is," Mr Evans would say.

His teacher would give him a thing so precious that he would always be grateful: musicianship.

It is the story as I heard it from Richard, maybe embellished a little, but in essence, true. To make the point that for a boy from a poor background, born with a driving force, the key would be his voice.

A boy soprano's voice is a tender thing. It breaks. But singing is more than voice. It is a thousand things that make it what it becomes... And Mr Evans gave that to Thomas.

Counterpoint, sight reading, chordal structure, transposing... all these he hammered into the boy's head. And the boy? He grew. He became confident. He even made a little money to help by singing in better-off houses around Manchester. He became known, much to his annoyance, as 'The Ernest Lough of the North' after the well-known boy soprano in the south.

Nothing much changed otherwise. Manchester was a grim, dirty place, those smogs (as they were called) hanging like ghosts in the air. The family had migrated from Wales during the depression, taking what work there was. Thomas lived with his mother and father and sister Vera in the two-up and two-down little house in a long-cobbled street. Money was always tight. The day the rent collector came was a bad day. But the road where they lived was a close-knit one. If help was needed, neighbours would always rally round.

Father went off to the railway each day. He worked in the signals. It was hard work. But employment was scarce, and a job was important. His mother, Mary, cleaned homes and offices, scraping enough together to pay for Thomas's singing lessons. She didn't know what she wanted for her son—a local teacher maybe. But she was a Welsh woman through and through. And to the Welsh, singing, the human voice, is part of their DNA. Could she ever have imagined where his voice would take him?

Mary Thomas: a typical Welsh matriarch ruled the household with a strong hand. In a drawer beside her chair was a cane. She took no disputes. What she said went in the tiny house. Richard slept in his parents' bedroom. Vera had the second bedroom with husband David. There was a bathroom on the ground floor, but the bath was usually where the coal was kept. Every morning, David, the son-in-law, would get up at six am, light the fire, then take a cup of tea to Vera.

Father Thomas would set off to work.

"I would hear his footsteps as he walked along. He walked with a regular rhythm," Richard would say. "I would be home

15

by the time he came back at night. I would listen for those footsteps."

His father, a mild-mannered gentle man, never questioned that Mary ruled. He just went along with it. Everyone in the family did. It was easier that way. Was he happy? His son was never sure.

"Sometimes I would hear him quietly weeping in bed at night."

Mary and Thomas Thomas came from a long line of Welsh people. Mary's family had lived in a small house called Plas Bach in Llansantssaid now in Powys. There her father had plied his trade as a shoe maker. Like many Welsh people, Richard felt his roots strongly. Every summer, the family would spend time in their old village visiting family, attending the tiny Welsh chapel that lay on the outskirts of the village. They were staunch and rigid Calvinistic Methodists.

Thomas remembered singing there.

"The minister was a typical Methodist preacher. He used what is called the huaual, a singsong declaiming from the Bible. Very passionate, very frightening sometimes, how God would strike you down if you didn't behave. That had a big effect on me."

One summer, we all went to Wales to see the village where both Richard's parents had lived. It was difficult to find—very small on the map. We wandered for some while. Then Vera wanted to spend a penny. Where to find somewhere? We decided to go into a farmyard and see if they would let us use their toilet. I stayed in the car while the others went inside. As I sat waiting, the farmer came out. I told him why we were here, about the chapel.

"Your husband is a singer then?" he asked.

"He is, yes"

"Would I know him then?"

I told him Richard's name.

"Oh, my goodness, your husband is our family favourite. We always listen when he sings on the radio… my mother will be over the moon."

That meant tea meeting mother, the afternoon passing. Soon we left, leaving one family with enough to boast about to their neighbours for a long time.

Richard Lewis with his mother, Mary

Eventually, we found the village and his mother's house. His father's house had long gone.

The House 'Plas Bach'

They say you should never visit the past. This was different. It was a memory. For Mary and Thomas Thomas had left Wales to find work all these years ago, leaving the place of their ancestors forever. Here was that past in front of a son and grandchildren, to them just an old bit of history, but they would remember.

We all congregated outside the house looking in, until the owner came out.

"Can I help you?"

I apologised for staring, "My husband's family used to live here many years ago."

"Indeed... what were the names then?"

"The name was Lewis."

"Oh, yes indeed. I have a Lewis on the deeds. I believe a son became a famous singer."

"Well, yes... and that's him there."

We were all invited into tea. Another tea! Not to be refused. As we walked up the path, I noticed little bits of leather lying in the grass. I drew the owner's attention to them.

"I've always wondered about them," she said.

I told her that Richard's grandfather had been a shoe maker.

"I expect that hut at the top was his shoe maker's shop."

She was delighted to be told. We went in. As we came out, I didn't want another cup of tea for a long time!

But back to where we were. Thomas was singing locally, getting a reputation.

Then one day, a letter from an agent in London arrived:

"Dear Thomas, would you be able to sing the part of the boy in Mendelssohn's *Elijah* in the Free Trade Hall with Isobel Baillie?"

Isobel Baillie! The top oratorio singer of the day.

"Oh, Thomas. What an honour."

The whole family and all the neighbours went to hear him. Local papers liked 'Local Boy'.

Baillie was very kind. "That was lovely dear," she said when it was over. "You have a beautiful voice."

But time was passing. Thomas was nearly fourteen. He knew that soon would come the dreaded day when his voice would break. But like all things we dread, he put worries aside.

One day came another letter:

"Would you come for an audition to the BBC?"

Going to London, now that was terrifying. Mr Evans said he would go with him.

Thomas couldn't sleep the night before. The whole family couldn't either. Maybe Mr Evans couldn't too.

The morning came. Thomas got up.

His voice had gone.

Mr Evans rushed over. "Bad luck that is. But now young man, no singing for at least two years or until the voice has settled."

Two years! Eternity that must have been.

Chapter Three

"I found it hard. But I wanted to be a tenor so passionately it was worth waiting for. I cheated sometimes. Public toilets had terrific resonance, so I would belt out a few notes just to hear myself. I began to think that maybe I was."

And he wasn't idle. Music studies continued. He was growing still. He was quite a lad with local girls… With his height and good looks, he was becoming a bit of a Romeo. But singing was never far away.

"Walking to work, I would see how many steps I could take without breathing."

He was always sure that his phenomenal breath control was partly because of those exercises.

Finally, the two years ended.

"Now, Thomas, Let's see what voice you have."

Rarely do good boy sopranos become good grown-up singers. No one really knows why. But it's a fact. So with what trepidation did Mr Evans have as his pupil opened his mouth to sing.

"Ee by gum, you're a tenor lad."

So, the work began. The past years had turned him into a musician, now the vocal work.

Thomas was seventeen. He had left school at fifteen and was working in a clothing factory which he hated.

"Was that it", he thought? Would he be forever stuck in grim Manchester with its pea soup fogs and the drudgery of a hated job? He could see no way out.

He wanted so much. He was handsome. The girls went for him. He had girlfriends. But they were only casual.

"I wanted more than that."

One day, the great Gigli came to town. Thomas bought a seat in the front row. Here was a singer that fulfilled every ambition... he couldn't wait to hear him, soak up what it was to be a professional.

"When Gigli walked out, I was a bit disappointed," he told me. "He was short, rather ugly with very little charisma. But then he began to sing. I listened as he poured out effortless legato phrases, heard the Italian language live for the first time, saw how he presented himself. I knew what I had to do."

At the stage door, Gigli shook his hand.

"I am studying to be a tenor, Signor Gigli."

"Come to sing for me next time I come."

He never came back. But Thomas had learned something.

Later, he went to hear Richard Tauber. Now here was a tenor that would become his ideal. Great singer, conductor, composer, musician... all the things that he wanted to be, what he thought of becoming. From then on, Thomas put Tauber at the top of his list.

Eighteen came, Nineteen, Twenty. He was still nowhere. Well known in his area, singing with the local operatic society and the choral society, getting some experience, but a seemingly hopeless possibility of getting away, making singing his life.

Richard Lewis singing with the Local Operatic Society

"I would sit in the office and look out over the grey roofs of Manchester and wonder if I would ever leave."

There was little help from government then.

Even winning the gold medal in the Associated Board exams failed to do anything—the first singer ever to do. But does light shine in the end?

Mr Evans had been busy. "Thomas, you have won a scholarship to the Royal Northern School of Music."

At last! He could fly. He could study. He could get away. Everything changed.

Now, he would find out if he had what it takes. Was he as good as he thought? Would it end as soon as it started? He was soon to find out.

His new teacher at the college was Norman Allin, a wonderful bass singer and a great teacher, who told me:

"I never had to do much. He was a natural singer, full of pent-up passion."

Marjorie Thomas was a fellow student, "I knew when I heard him, he would reach starry heights."

How happy Thomas was, but Norman Allin had something to say about his name. In the Welsh tradition, first sons took their father's name and the surname... hence two Thomas's. His father and his grandfather had been Thomas Thomas.

"Thomas Thomas! You can't have a career with a name like that. Find another one."

A new name? To be born again! But what? His mother was a Lewis. That might do. He admired Richard Tauber. Richard Lewis... that sounded OK. So, Richard Lewis he became.

But life does not always go along as you want.

This was 1939. Rumours were in the air. War was talked about. He heard the rumours. It couldn't happen to him! It couldn't! Not when he was just getting on with his dream. But it did. One morning, a letter came from the war office to attend recruitment. So now a problem: Thomas (or Richard now) was a pacifist. Brought up in a strong Methodist religion, it was against all his beliefs.

"You can join the Royal Signals or go to prison."

Choice? Not really. He joined the Royal Signals.

"I realised how wrong I was pretty soon."

Chapter Four

For our story, I leap ahead. Why? Because dreams were demolished? Our story over before it began?

I only learned how terrible it was for him after he had died. He talked about it, of course, but when I read his diaries, I could see… I had always known he was a prolific diary keeper. Every day of his life, he wrote something. But the years from when he was called up to the day of his demob… blank. Nothing. To me that said it all. They were the years that had come to stop his journey.

He'd had no choice, of course. The country was in peril. All young men knew they had to endure what was to come. Richard was no exception.

But maybe he had a guardian angel.

During his time with the Royal Signals, he had some hair-raising experiences, avoiding a near death one. His unit had been ordered to go to the front. His sergeant decided to keep Richard back to see if any messages came through. That morning, their jeep had a direct hit, and all the men were killed.

And it was not all awful. He sang with ENSA, that famous troop entertainment organisation where many a career began. He even sang in the same programme as Vera Lynn, and one act he remembered:

"A chap who played violins of every size, between his legs."

But let's jump to 1945: the end of the war, demob. It was over. Now he could get on, but how? He was no more forward in his ambition than before. Was all this for nothing?

There had been one bit of good fortune. During the war, his commanding officer was a woman who soon realised that this young soldier could be utilised better than giving him a gun, so she sent him as an army ambassador, in uniform, to sing mainly in Brussels and Norway. There he sang Benjamin Britten works: *Les Illuminations, Nocturne, Serenade for Tenor, Horn and Strings*

A young soldier singing in army uniform went down well with people, and he was getting some good experience, singing with orchestras for the first time in his life.

Richard Lewis singing with The Oslo Philharmonic Orchestra in Army Uniform

He was learning to embrace a new world as well. It would be easy to forget that he had not long ago been stuck in grimy Manchester. It was as if the clouds of despair and self-doubts had gone. This is what he wanted, what he could do well, experiencing what it was like to be admired, applauded for the first time.

So his five years in the army were not entirely wasted, even if he thought they had been. How could he have thought otherwise? Time was passing. When he should have been experimenting and learning, he was marooned in an army uniform!

Bits of luck came his way: an extraordinary meeting out of the blue.

After a concert in Oslo, a man came to him: "Would you like to meet Kirsten Flagstad?"

The great soprano had a house up in the mountains. Richard was invited to dinner. She had heard about this young soldier and was curious.

"It was unreal," he told me, "for after dinner, when she had kindly asked about my singing, she got up, and for the rest of the evening, she sang song after song, standing by a window looking out over the fjords."

Later on, he had an opportunity to sing in Purcell's *Dido and Aeneas* with her in London but was unable to accept, to his disappointment. She came to see him in his dressing room at Covent Garden:

"I had not heard you sing, but somehow knew you would get on in the profession."

His demob had taken forever to come. Finally, he was free. Five years had come to an end. And little did he know, but an enormous bit of luck was about to happen.

For news of this singing soldier came to the ears of Benjamin Britten, the English composer.

An agent in Brussels had written:

"I would like to recommend an excellent tenor who has been singing your works here with great success and who is, incidentally, good to look at."

Britten was maybe curious to meet this tenor who was good to look at, but more importantly, the composer was searching for a second tenor to Peter Pears.

Richard did not yet know about this development. He was in London. He went to the Royal Academy of Music. Could he become a student? He was thirty-two by now, mature to start studying again.

The Academy had written: "I'm afraid you are too old to join the Academy," was the response to his application.

Norman Allin had other ideas, and Richard began his studies.

"I wasn't going to let this singer go. My gut instinct knew he had a destiny," Allan would say.

Was that going to be the end of it?

No, it was the beginning. For the phone rang one morning:

"Would Mr Lewis please arrange to sing to Mr Britten?"

Then another phone call: "Would Mr Lewis please come and sing to Glyndebourne?"

And if that was not enough, he had a request to sing to David Webster at Covent Garden.

Evidently, it had got around that there was an exceptional singer in London, and at that time, exceptional singers, particularly tenors, were short on the ground.

So like a seismic upheaval, things accelerated almost too fast.

In a matter of weeks, he was booked at Covent Garden, at Glyndebourne to sing with Benjamin Britten's English Opera Group, at the same time taking classes and having singing lessons at the Academy. A unique state of affairs!

A magical turn of events? Had all his dreams come true at once?

He must have thought so. Or was he so sure of his destiny? Yes, I think so, from what he told me.

If you think as you read it that it should be impossible to go from obscurity to where he had got to an impossible dream, yet he did. Circumstance, opportunity, whatever it was, Richard, almost overnight, had done it.

Of course, not all things were good... but it was a start. I found myself in the company of Karl Rankl, David Webster, Kathleen Ferrier, Nancy Evans, Peter Pears, Joan Cross. We all gathered in Britten's London flat to read through *Albert Herring*.

Heady stuff indeed! "We would sit on the floor as Ben played through the score. We all knew that something amazing was happening. If I tried to look nonchalant, it hid my excitement to know I was part of this new company."

He had also married Mary, daughter of the first flute in the Halle orchestra. They found a flat in London. They had a son, Michael, now my much-loved stepson. He was in the thick of the London music scene. And he now did something he had promised himself. He was working on his Manchester accent. Nowadays, that wouldn't be a problem; then it was a drawback. And he did have a strong one. None of the musical Welsh lilt that his parents had. It was pure Mancunian, hard and ugly. Gradually, he ironed it out; only seen in a glimpse if you listen to him singing in English.

I doubt if many singers we know today could have risen in such a meteoric way. Compared with the long training taken for granted today, he was, relatively untrained, certainly, in stage craft. One day, unknown with little prospect of going anywhere, the next, almost overnight, part of the most important opera company in the country.

The English Opera Group was based at Glyndebourne. The excitement everyone must have felt! Not only at last able to get on with careers after five years, but working on, as yet, unknown but thrilling new operas. It was the stuff that dreams are made of.

And he had to learn fast. It might have daunted a less confident man, but he had waited a long time for it. No way would he waste this opportunity.

He was now part of it, second tenor to Peter Pears.

The country had suffered but the war was over now, and an energy engulfed the country.

And the newly named Richard Lewis was right in the middle.

He began touring the country with Britten's operas, getting rave notices, learning his art, finding out what he could do best. His capacity for learning roles would one day become legendary: tales of extraordinary feats of memory. Taking over the role of the Prince in *Boris Godunov* with twenty-four hours' notice. *Billy Budd* after twenty years not singing it, relearned in an evening on the train from London. Tippett's *Child of our Time* for a BBC film, learned on the train to the studio. His capacity for incredibly fast learning was soon part of a reputation that would follow him. If you wanted a singer who could learn something with little time to do so, he would be the first singer to come to mind.

What gave him this extraordinary gift of learning quickly? Several elements. The first was a photographic memory; he could see the score. Then his outstanding musicianship. And this quality plus that voice precipitated him into world-class music.

The years of hard work under Mr Evans would bear fruit that not even Evans could have envisaged. He had languished in army uniform longing for something out of his reach. Something he thought had been snatched from him. Could he have dreamed of all this?

"I have to admit it was almost unbelievable."

So, he was now steeping himself in music, learning new roles, part of this exciting new opera project. Did it go smoothly? Does everything always go smoothly?

In this case, a very potent one: Peter Pears was Benjamin Britten's lover.

That meant that Britten would never give priority to another tenor. All first performances would be sung by Pears. Richard understood that. But the atmosphere was pretty precious. On the other hand, he had been given this chance. After all, it was launching his career. Until... Something happened that would set alarm bells ringing.

He was due to sing *The Rape of Lucretia* at Glyndebourne (Nancy Evans as Lucretia). It was to be broadcast. This would be Richard's first. Naturally, he was happy. His name would be in the Radio Times for the first time. Opening it, he was disappointed to see Peter Pears listed.

He went to see Britten.

"Ben, I thought I was singing in that performance?"

"Yes, you are. Just wasn't sure if you would be ready in time, Richard"

Anyone who worked with him knew this could not be true.

Eric Crozier, the director told him, "Your top notes are better than Peter's, Richard. He doesn't like that."

Things were not much better when at one performance of *Lucretia* Richard muddled up a dialogue, "Rome was now ruled by the Italian upstart," which came out as, "Rome was now ruled by the Italian dustcart." Britten never forgave him.

But the experience of touring, singing night after night, was a perfect training ground.

And he seems to have done rather well. Reviews of the time:

Peter Grimes in Birmingham:

"Richard Lewis has made the role of Grimes very much his own."

"Richard Lewis' Grimes is by now an all-time standard for the part."

Elizabeth Muir-Lewis

Richard Lewis singing Peter in Peter Grimes by Benjamin Britten

Albert Herring:

"Richard Lewis is quite as funny as Fernandel, the French film star."

Another wrote, "I recommend *Herring* at least as three time as strongly as I have ever recommended any opera performance in Birmingham."

But the warning bells had resoundingly sounded. He soon realised that he would never progress by staying with Britten. By now he was singing *Peter Grimes* at Covent Garden, *Così fan Tutte* at Sadler's Wells, recitals and oratorio around the country, and had an agent, Emmie Tillett.

So he left. But it had not been wasted. He had been able to work closely with Benjamin Britten.

"Among the finest conductors and accompanists, I ever knew."

The time had come to leave.

The journey went on. Nothing could stop him now.

What sort of fees was he getting? For a *Messiah*: £25. His first *Dream of Gerontius* with Sir Malcolm Sargent: £30. Doesn't sound much, but in 1946–7, it was pretty good.

This is a tale of a time of great artists, conductors, producers, composers. When the relevance of opera was not questioned as it is today. Psychological overtones not agonised over. There was no time for that. We, like the rest of the western world, had to find our way again. The Second World War had not been over long. With it came huge rising of energy, and that energy was about to create a monumental rising of the arts in this country,

There were old problems to surmount.

Opera, at that time in this country, was mostly, if not all, sung in English. Was now the time when we would finally enter the world of world-class singing? And there was one extraordinary opera house, that had opened in the 30s which would lead the way.

Glyndebourne

Why did this tiny country opera house end up changing our operatic history? We had never had an operatic tradition. Operas by Handel and Purcell,—that was about the limit of opera in England.

We had not sung in languages. There were not many British singers of world status. It would be Richard and others who would change that.

Before the war, there had been Heddle Nash, Eva Turner, Roy Henderson.

A gradual transformation began. It was a painful one, but from the end of the war onwards, we began to grow and learn. Now international artists such as Bryn Terfel, Thomas Allen match any artists from anywhere in the musical world—the product of those early singing pioneers if you like. It didn't happen overnight.

And much of it, if not all of it, was the Glyndebourne influence. Every season, foreign singers would arrive singing in their own language. British singers had to hurry up, to learn, to listen. All the operas were to be in the original language, not in translation.

We all know the story of Glyndebourne. How it was created. The inspiration? John Christie: a small dynamic man, an eccentric, a man who would not take no for an answer, an extraordinary character who would passionately bring to fruition his dream.

John Christie, with (from the left), daughter Rosamund, daughter in law Mary and son George.

John Christie
Founder of Glyndebourne Opera

The son of a 'Landed Gentry' family who had this lovely house set in rolling Sussex hills, spawned, quite against the usual upper-class ways, a man who was passionate about opera, particularly Wagner. Had he married a Wagnerian singer, we would have had a mini-Bayreuth in Sussex. But he didn't. He met and married Audrey Mildmay, a singer, a very good light soprano, ideal for Mozart. The opera house was built was for Audrey, where she sang for five seasons.

John Christie had this driving desire to put on opera in his home, and he was something else: a classic eccentric. Tales of his eccentricities are legendary.

Critics called him mad. Perhaps he was. Didn't he have to be? Putting on opera in a small Sussex garden; which had a loss of several thousand after the first season? And did not deter him. Very little did. From the beginning, there were big ideas. He was the driving force. Behind him was always Audrey. "If you are going to do it John," she is known to have said, "do it properly."

And that is what he did. Employing the best that Europe could give him.

Around him, he gathered a band of great musicians who would set the parameters for the new opera house.

He was lucky in a way, for he had the opportunity to invite many outstanding musicians to Glyndebourne who were leaving or fleeing their country as Nazism took hold in Europe: Fritz Busch, Carl Ebert, Jani Strasser, Peter Gellhorn, Paul Hamburger, Martin Isepp.

So, what of Richard; how does he figure in the Glyndebourne story? From the start, he was embraced by the company, given roles that would keep him loyal to them for over forty years, a home, a place to grow artistically. For when he began, he had had little acting experience. At Glyndebourne, he would have Dr Carl Ebert as his mentor. This great German actor-turned-producer was an outstanding, stunningly handsome man who reigned for many years. Some of the greatest Glyndebourne productions were his: *Così fan*

Tutte, *Rake's Progress*, *Alceste*, *Rosenkavalier*, among countless others.

Among the musicians was someone that would be of great importance for the future of the company, and exert huge influence: Jani Strasser, Head of Music for many years. Who told me:

"I came to see an opera house in the garden of this extraordinary eccentric, meaning to just visit. I saw, I heard, and stayed for forty years."

Jani Strasser in the Prompt Box

The Story
(As Told to Me by Jani)

"I was a singing teacher in Vienna. One day, I got a message that a Mr Christie from England wanted to meet me. I had no idea who this was but agreed. He came to my apartment. I opened the door. There stood this extraordinary man, a top hat on plus fours, with a pug under his arm. 'I am building an opera house in my garden,' he announced, 'would you come and be my music director?'"

"What did you do, Jani?" I asked.

"I just forgot about him. He had to be mad. Until a phone call came, 'Where are you?' said an autocratic voice. This was after nearly six months So I took up his invitation to go and see this little opera house in the country, with no hope that it was anything but some mad scheme thought up by an eccentric aristocrat."

"What happened when you got there?"

"After three days of touring the site, hearing what Mr Christie planned, I realised that here, maybe, just maybe, was an operatic utopia. In many ways it was. The aims of this man's ambitions, backed up by his wife, certainly excited me."

He was not alone. Many great musicians fell for Christie's dream: Carl Ebert, Fritz Bush and Peter Gellhorn. He and countless others were why Glyndebourne became what it is today. Refugees from Nazi Germany, they found a home, a musical haven; saw the possibilities that perfect music could be made. In particular, Mozart. It was what every musician dreams of: ideal conditions to realise, what are often, lifetime hopes. Christie made their dreams come true.

Of course, its start had problems. Most people and, in particular, critics, thought the whole idea was mad. "Opera in a field," cried one, "Opera in a barn," cried another.

The first performance of *Figaro* in 1934 had very few in the audience. However, critics thought that maybe here was something interesting. The next performance had a few more in the audience.

Until it was suspected that something extraordinary was happening. The rest, as the saying goes, is history.

So what were the components that made up this new venture?

The orchestra, with its fine musicians: A local orchestra was not good enough for Mr Christie. It had to be the best. The Royal Philharmonic Orchestra first played for Glyndebourne in Edinburgh in 1948

The foreign singers who set the precedent of coming, rehearsing, relaxing. Maybe they too came wondering how an opera house in a country garden could possibly be worth their time, but gave it a go. Then found something not found anywhere else. Not even today. For while it has got bigger, has a new building, it is in essence the same.

And what about John Christie: the great joker who loved to play tricks, one of England's great eccentrics.

To give you an example of those eccentricities: one afternoon, a final rehearsal was taking place of *Così fan Tutte*.

Richard was Ferrando. He decided to go out and have a cigarette, leaning against the wall just outside the stage door. Mr Christie came round with a group of guests. He introduces Richard (in costume and make-up) as his head gardener. And Richard played along. It was expected!

The Film Maker Tenor

Richard Lewis plays Nero in The Crowning of
Poppea by Monteverdi

Once when Mr Christie was doing some gardening, a
group of strangers came up to him to ask him something,
thinking he was the gardener, not realising that it was the
owner himself. They ended up going to the opera that evening
as his guests.

Mr Christie was notably a rather wayward driver. If he
decided to drive over to Lewes, the local police were notified
and the roads were cleared for him.

But whatever his extraordinary ways, what he did was magnificent and that he began something that has flourished and is bigger and self-sustaining.

One stipulation at the beginning, which has been maintained to this day, was the dress code: ladies in evening dress and gents in black tie. If any patron dared to arrive not properly dressed (in his eyes) Mr Christie would send them home! The dress code has become of course a lot more casual. Ball gowns a thing of the past and the smell of mothballs as dowagers passed, but it is still a magic world of make believe.

The picnics, the lawns littered with baskets overflowing with lobster and champagne, umbrellas in different colours, women in their silks and satins—a tradition from the very beginning, all part of the Glyndebourne experience.

Yes, it was the place where wealth and privilege sometimes seemed to be prevalent, but it was, and is, the place where ordinary people come to enjoy the unique atmosphere and enjoy superb music.

I guess that Mr Christie took great pleasure in doing things that were mischievous, such as going round the toilets after the performance turning off the lights.

Toilets were an important detail. For instance, the singers' toilets had special designs that would accommodate artistes in their large skirts. The roll call of singers was impressive in those early years. They came from all over the world to make music in this unusual setting.

Singers at that time were Roy Henderson, Heddle Nash, Norman Allin, Willi Domgraf-Fassbaender, Ina Souez, Walther Ludwig and John Brownlee, among others. They were the mainstay of the 1934–1935 seasons. Later came Dino Borgioli, Norman Walker, David Franklin... a bit later came Risë Stevens, Salvatore Baccaloni, David Lloyd, Mariano Stabile. In all the productions, Audrey Mildmay sang in five seasons and three productions between 1934 and 1939.

She had a lovely silvery soprano. History tells us that she was adamant that she would not sing if Jani Strasser did not think she was good enough. She had come from the Carl Rosa opera, so she was experienced. But knowing that she would be criticised as John Christie's wife, this she insisted on. Jani approved, and she would sing for many years.

Dino Borgioli, one of the singers who came to Glyndebourne, had been important to Richard. During the war, he had had some singing lessons from the Italian, paying him in cigarettes (valuable commodities in war time).

For a singer like Richard, as with other performers, Glyndebourne provided a huge opportunity. Not only were rehearsals long and intense, but were relaxed and friendly with the opportunity to study roles in depth.

As English musical life began developing, other places began to think about what to do. So it is not surprising that Edinburgh turned its thoughts to putting on a festival. I am not certain if the Edinburgh folklore's claim that Mrs John Christie, during a tour of Gay's *Beggar's Opera*, remarked to Rudolf Bing what a great place it could be to have a festival was true. But so the story goes, and Rudi Bing, (later to run the Met in New York) then Glyndebourne's artistic director, took this up, envisaging something like the Salzburg Festival, with the magnificent setting of the castle towering over the city as a focal point. Whoever it was, it certainly bore fruit. It opened on 24th of August 1947.

The Glyndebourne company would appear that year with Mozart's *Nozze di Figaro*.

One of the first *Don Giovanni's* there in the early years had an impressive cast list: Ljuba Welitsch, Paolo Silveri, David Franklin, Hilde Gueden, Ian Wallace and Richard.

And what about Benjamin Britten's English Opera Group which had made a home in Glyndebourne just after the war? Unfortunately, he and John Christie fell out, and he stopped using the house. It was said that Mr Christie did not like Britten's music.

Looking at the list of singers who came back year after year, it was a company that looked for new names, creating a firm and close relationship for everyone. Initially, Mrs Christie arranged for the singers to sleep in the main house. This ultimately caused a problem as many of the singers swopped bedrooms!

For a singer like Richard, it was operatic sanctuary: time to rehearse, relax, learn new roles under the finest coaches. With coaching from people like Jani Strasser, soon he was recognised as a fine Mozartian singer.

Zauberflöte in Dublin, the critic wrote:

"This is finest Mozart tenor since before the war. His mellifluous singing reminds me of John McCormac at his best. An Irishman cannot say better than that."

The list of singers in 1950 were names that continued to sing with the company for years: Geraint Evans, Murray Dickie, Erich Kunz, Sena Jurinac, Blanche Thebom, Alda Noni, George London, April Cantelo, Marjorie Thomas, Douglas Craig, Alexander Young and Owen Brannigan.

Richard Lewis sings Tamino in the Magic Flute by Mozart at Glyndebourne

Richard Lewis and Joan Sutherland in Don Giovanni by Mozart in The San Francisco Opera

From the left, Richard Lewis, Victoria de Los Angeles and Ilva Ligabue, in Don Giovanni at The San Francisco Opera.

Before the new bar and theatre was built, there was an old bar—not very big, basic, but beloved of the artists (and the public for that matter). So many memories of that draughty place found at the foot of the stairs, where the wind blew on a wet night and a tarpaulin flapped.

One evening after a performance, we were introduced to Sir Laurence Olivier. I found myself alone with him, both of us propping up the bar. It was surreal really, for he had been my idol. But there I was, and I took the opportunity to talk about acting in opera as opposed to the straight stage.

What would such a great actor think of opera's restrictions on movement and emotion? To my surprise, he was complimentary about the acting that night, expressing admiration that anyone could sing and act at the same time!

Funnily enough, that was echoed by what a well-known actress (Dame Judi Dench) said to me as we both queued in the loo one night. Now we take it for granted. But I suppose it is hard to combine the two art forms. In my lifetime, I have seen this change. In the early days, such as when Handel's operas were all the rage, tales of singers, large, fat and static and temperamental, now gone (mostly).

But what of our tenor?

By now, he was well established into English musical life… in great demand. He had become one of the major singers in the country. All sorts of carrots were waiting to happen. Not least one big one *The Dream of Gerontius* by Edward Elgar.

The Dream of Gerontius
By Edward Elgar

When he was a soldier dreaming of the life, he thought had slipped away from him, one work that would constantly be in his head was Elgar's *Dream of Gerontius*.

He felt he was ideal, never thinking he would sing it, and never dreaming that one day he would be considered one of the greatest interpreters of this difficult role.

How wrong he would be.

Fortunately for him, there were two conductors at that time who loved the work: Sir Malcolm Sargent and Sir John Barbirolli. Richard had by now begun to work with both of them and so was inevitably booked to sing the work. And he had been right. His voice was ideal. His religious Methodist upbringing, in spite of the work being Catholic (Cardinal Newman), lent him sympathy for the emotions depicted by Elgar.

Very soon, he was the Gerontius of his time. Taking over the mantle (as Malcolm Sargent would say) from Heddle Nash.

His first *Gerontius* was with Sargent in 1949 in Liverpool... just four years after the war had ended.

Chapter Five
The History of Gerontius

Gerontius has a special history. Ever since 1900 when it was first heard in the Birmingham Festival with Edward Lloyd as Gerontius, it has held a special place in British musical life, he was followed by Gervaise Elwes in this part.

Passed from tenor to tenor, over the years, the mantle of Gerontius became a prize to be won. From Elwes it passed to Heddle Nash and then to Richard Lewis

Many tenors have sung it. But Richard Lewis had a special quality that would mark him out as the finest of his generation. He had the power: depth of range as well as a thrilling top. He could spin an exquisite line in pianissimo with magical beauty.

His first performance was with Sir Malcolm Sargent in Liverpool in February 1949.

John Amis, the critic, was in the audience that night.

"We knew a new Gerontius had risen," he told me.

Sir John Barbirolli also booked him for it. He wrote:

"Ever since our Gerontius together in Leeds, I have been wanting to send you a word to tell you I was deeply touched by your singing of the part. It will mature in time. But I feel you have it in you to become the finest Gerontius of your generation. It was deeply sensitive, musical and musicianly."

That was written in 1950. In 1951, he wrote again:

"May I make a little request to you before Saturday's *Dream*. There is one place I am not happy with. It is the phrase in part two, number twenty, beginning 'I ever believed' which always to me seemed to be too fast for the particular expression. If you try it with a metronome you can see that a crotchet equals fifty-four. It seems a bit slow, but I think that indicates what Elgar wanted. Also, can you make 'Under the awful presence of God' a little darker in sound if possible. Many thanks and looking forward to your beautiful performance again."

What grace and elegance!

So those longings and certainty that this work was for him were proved to be right.

He would record it twice, with ten years between the two.

Of the first Sargent recording (with Marjorie Thomas) *Gramophone* magazine wrote: "There is no one in this class."

Ten years later, the Barbirolli recording (with Janet Baker), *Record and Recordings* wrote: "It is fascinating to compare the two recordings to see how Lewis's interpretation has matured. The earlier performance, though eloquent and superbly articulated, lacks the dynamic range of the new one."

I was at the recording sessions in Manchester. It was a typical Manchester day: thick fog, drizzle. Not a day to raise the spirits, particularly Richard's. It must have seemed like the past had returned! Kim Borg was truly miserable. Janet Baker her usual calm self. Sir John directed in his slippers. I doubt he felt inspired by such a day. Result: a terrific recording.

Of the two recordings—they were re-issued on CD—Richard could listen to both. He always loved singing with Marjorie Thomas. She was a warm lovely person.

Marjorie told me a tale once. She had sung the work with him many times. One day he took her aside, "Marjorie, you should sing it from memory."

"And you know, he was absolutely right."

Janet Baker and he also sang together many times. Here and in America. A different generation, but colleagues in sympathy with each other. If I felt, as he did, that Marjorie was the more sympathetic Angel, that did not take from Janet's superb singing of the role.

So how were English singers faring in the scheme of things? Had that renaissance after the war produced some good voices?

There is no doubt we had a crop of superb singers.

Geoffrey Thompson certainly thought so. He wrote:

"IS THERE A NEW GOLDEN AGE? For it is evident we are producing singers equal to any."

He goes on to name singers who were at the forefront of our music scene. Singers David Ward, the fine Scottish bass, Josephine Veasey, Peter Pears, Alexander Young, Amy Shuard, Gwyneth Jones, Michael Langdon, Elsie Morison, Heather Harper, Monica Sinclair, Geraint Evans, Peter Glossop, and of course, Richard.

The writer goes on:

"The role of Gerontius has had several exponents. I missed the first one (Elwes)(sic) but I have heard them all. The best of them is, in my opinion, Richard Lewis—in sheer quality of voice, vocal technique, musicianship, feeling and taste. Here moreover is a tenor equally capable of Mozart,

Handel, Bach, Britten, Mahler, Sullivan and Schoenberg, bringing to all a mellifluous tone and immaculate style. With respect to Heddle Nash, we produced between the wars no tenor of this calibre and versatility."

Did these singers begin the onward march of this country rivalling those from the rest of the world? A country that had been devoid of international singers, except for a few, now had its own school of singers who would encompass the world.

So I must go back again to the end of the war again, when the artistic life of London had more or less ground to a halt. We had to pick ourselves up. This took time. And we did. If there is one thing the national spirit has, it's this ability to get together and start again.

Glyndebourne had closed, using the house for evacuee children. Very little opera was heard. Heroes and heroines of those years are still remembered. Dame Myra Hess playing as the bombs fell, Malcolm Sargent with his orchestra (my father attended one). In the middle of the concert, the siren went off. Sargent turned to his audience:

"Please leave and go to a safe place if you wish to."

No one moved. Neither did the orchestra. That was in Queens Hall. Which I believe was bombed not long after…

In 1945, a new energy had galvanised the musical life of the country.

And Richard Lewis was in the centre of it.

You might ask what was it that this tenor had or did that made him so much in demand?

I will try to answer as I saw it. And as a fellow singer, hope I lend weight to it.

First of all, beauty of voice. Phenomenal breath control. Superb diction. An ability to learn roles (he had a photographic memory which helped). Musicianship. An ability to make difficult music sound easy. An intellect that let him learn modern roles with ease... Which brings me nicely to his work with modern composers... Michael Tippett, William Walton, Igor Stravinsky, Luigi Nono, Elizabeth Maconachy, and Gisela Kleber... not forgetting Arnold Schönberg.

Chapter Six
Moses and Aaron
By Arnold Schönberg

Let me start with Schönberg. He of the twelve-tone music. Music so difficult, that even after many performances of *Moses and Aaron* in London, Boston and Paris, Richard would wonder how he learned it.

Covent Garden put it on. Sir Georg Solti conducting, Sir Peter Hall producing, John Bury the stage designer and a translation by David Rudkin, Forbes Robinson as Moses and Richard as Aaron, plus an enormous chorus.

The powers that be were sure the opera would be a commercial failure... how wrong they were! Yet no way could they have foreseen what would happen. It was hardly conventional English opera goings on!

The staging was designed to be fantastic: raw, bloody, an orgy, simulated sex, animal sacrifice, and half-naked girls, a huge chorus and three naked girls called virgins, played by strippers. Some of the chorus went overboard with the simulated sex or maybe they were just good actors! The animals gave some trouble. Stage staff had to be at the side of the stage with buckets.

Aaron had a staff that had to turn into a snake which did not work all the time. It caused him quite a bit of nervous energy every time the scene came. "Would it work tonight or just droop? It was a difficult moment every time I came to do it." He had a costume that looked like sacking, and did it stink! Very heavy, but looked authentic!

Richard Lewis sings Aaron in Schönberg's Moses & Aaron at Covent Garden, London.

Sir Georg Solti

As rehearsals got underway, matters began to develop unexpectantly. The press got wind of the naked virgins. Black market tickets were touted. The stage door had a phalanx of press with cameras, contributing to a bust up one afternoon after rehearsal. We came out to be besieged by flashing cameras, and shouts of, "Are the strippers coming out?"

Incensed, Richard was about to hit one of them on the nose (he could be volatile). I dashed into the theatre and got hold of Sir David Webster, who came down and calmed things.

Those were the days when the media were not so avid for scandal... otherwise, no doubt a headline in the Mail or Telegraph would read, "Tenor in fracas outside Covent Garden," or, "Naked strippers at Covent Garden cause a fight."

Further on in rehearsal, walking in for his first cue, Richard was faced with the three naked girls lying on the floor. "You might have told me," he shouted to Peter Hall. It was the only time I saw him unable to sing for a few minutes.

The back stage manager was Stella. She did not approve at all of naked girls. Every evening she would be waiting at the side of the stage with rugs to throw over them to hide their nudity from the rest of the cast.

Moses and Aaron would become one of the most controversial productions of the sixties.

The *Financial Times* wrote: "Perhaps no production since Beecham's *Elektra* has stimulated so much advance attention."

A tabloid wrote: "I went to an orgy last night. For £1.11.6p, I saw blood, gore, strippers and music. It was a good orgy— wine, slaughter, raw meat, drunkenness, human sacrifice, phallic symbolism and gallons of blood."

Evening News: "Well, it's here! The achievement on the whole is a triumph that will send the fame of Covent Garden around the world."

The Mail: "Richard Lewis achieved miracles of eloquent expression as Aaron. Forbes Robinson makes a fine wild-looking Moses, but Richard Lewis deserves even more congratulations—sailing through difficulties while making the result as easy as Aaron himself."

The Times: "This was stupendous. I doubt if there is anything like it in the history of Covent Garden."

Joyce Grenfell: "I liked it. I must go back sometime to hear the music."

Solti liked it so much he put it on in Paris, this time in French. Richard again Aaron, and a French actor doing the speaking part of Moses, which did not work as well as Forbes Robinson's bass voice had resonated so well in the *Sprechstimme* (speaking voice) For this, the singer had to speak the text in time with the music, a most difficult art, but against the singing of Aaron, very effective.

Richard learned it again in French. Solti was worried. Why? That Richard's diction was so good that if his French was bad it would be criticised. Not one French critic made any derogatory comments about his French. One English critic did though! Surprise, surprise!

Another *Moses* was put on in Boston, directed by another eccentric, Sarah Caldwell. This extraordinary woman not only directed it but conducted it. She was a sort of John Christie in female form… totally obsessed, a real power house in her opera world. Her *Moses* set was unusual. A walkway had been built right round the orchestra. That meant that half the time the action took place behind the conductors back. Did it work? Maybe. Ambitious though.

Of other *Moses* the Covent Garden production was certainly the most ambitious: the most startling and the most talked about. The music? You wouldn't go out humming any tunes. But the total result was stupendous.

How lucky we were at that time to have a group of great composers: Michael Tippett, Lennox Berkeley, Herbert Howells, Ralph Vaughan Williams, Benjamin Britten and

William Walton. Could that be described as a 'riches' of composers'?

I was an assiduously loyal wife, knowing how important for an artist it is to have a friendly face in the audience. Maybe you could call it stamina! I managed thirteen *Moses and Aaron's*, both the Tippett operas, all the Walton *Troilus and Cressida's* here and in Australia. Not counting almost every other performance everywhere and anywhere.

So what did these composers think of each other?

I discovered too late that you should be careful what you say. At a party where Britten and Peter Pears were also there, in a conversation with a guest, I said something about Michael Tippett, to be told, "We do not mention him." Jealousy? Surely not. However, two composers in the same generation?

Another highlight in London's musical life was the first opera by Sir William Walton, called The Bear.

Troilus and Cressida

This wonderful opera caused a musical sensation when first heard. It went on to have a chequered history and is now rarely, if ever, heard,

Then it was a different story.

The premier was December 3rd 1954.

Critics said:

"Few achievements in the musical world have gained such universal acclaim as *Troilus and Cressida*. The atmosphere was tense with expectation and excitement, and soon established beyond all question that the new work will be among the greatest of our time."

Sir William Walton

Richard Lewis sings Troilus in Troilus & Cressida

Eric Blom wrote: "There need be no hesitation in saying at once that this is a great and most impressive work, one that we can exchange unblushingly with foreign operas we have adopted."

Another wrote: "Richard Lewis as Troilus had all the power, passion and beauty of voice that the part demanded. This was a towering performance."

"Richard Lewis knocks spots off Stewart Granger!"

"As Troilus, Richard Lewis becomes more like Marlon Brando every minute but retains his competent singing technique."

Not sure what the critic was getting at there!

"Richard Lewis will sing the part in America, the first British singer to be engaged by an American Opera Company since Eva Turner before the war."

The opera did well in America. Not everyone liked it though. One afternoon, Richard was relaxing on the roof of the San Francisco hotel, when Jussi Björling came and sat down beside him. They chatted for a while. Just before Björling left he commented, "I heard a rehearsal of the English opera. You know that you will never get on if you sing music like that."

The opera's history is unhappy. It bombed at La Scala. Then Covent Garden put it on with Janet Baker, the role of Cressida transposed down for Baker's voice. This did not work as the essence of Cressida's music is essentially the exciting high tessitura. So that seemed to put an end to the opera called 'The Greatest work of our time'. Such a pity. It is full of wonderful melodies, passionate, almost Puccini-like arias. Good character parts. Not modern, in the sense that it tried to say something new. It just had good powerful tunes.

Maybe that's why the critics did not like it? And maybe that was why in the end, it faded away. Do you always have to say something new if what you write is superb?

I was lucky to know Sir William Walton quite well. He was quite a ladies' man. We got on very well. I was always a good listener, and Sir William liked to talk.

One year we went over to Australia. 1964, I think it was, for we married in 1963 and it was not long after. The trip was a sort of honeymoon. The Adelaide Festival was on and one event was the Australian premier of Walton's opera. The cast was strong. Marie Collier sang Cressida. She was ideal: passionate, beautiful, sexy, singing the difficult soaring musical lines with tremendous confidence. She had a great success. "Local girl makes good…" for she was Australian.

I was sitting next to Sir William on the opening night.

In the opera, there is a section in which Cressida sings a *Scarf aria*. Marie came on; no scarf. She realised too late. I watched her. As she sang, she moved carefully stage right. A hand came out with a scarf. She took it and carried on. Sir William did not notice.

He was totally absorbed, living every moment of his creation. The mechanics held no interest.

Much later, I was with him in the BBC box at the Albert Hall when the *Troilus* love duets were sung by Jill Gomez and Richard in a Promenade concert. The duets were lovely. Turning to Sir William to say something, he was weeping.

"Are you all right, Sir William?"

"Thank you, my dear," he answered. "I had forgotten how beautiful they are."

We chatted when the concert was over.

"Composing is not easy," he told me. "What I write is in my head. I hear it when it is performed, and only then can I know if it has worked. And to hear it tonight, sung by top singers, that confirms it in my mind." He likened it to someone giving birth, "only then can you see the result."

Maybe someday *Troilus* will make a comeback. I hope so.

Chapter Seven
Adventure by the Sea

It was while we were in Adelaide, we got into a situation. Maybe you could call it an adventure.

On a performance day, we decided to get out of town and spend the day by the sea, leaving plenty time to get back.

Some friends lent us a car. We set off. Arriving at the resort, without thinking and not seeing a notice that said 'Don't drive onto the sand', we drove onto the sand. Not a good move. The sand was thick. The wheels sank down into it. To make things worse, Richard dropped the keys which disappeared, never to be seen again!

This beach was not like an English one. It was vast, no one there. Absolutely empty except for a man in a van the far end, so far away we could hardly see him, like a Lowry pin man! I waved, screamed. He saw me eventually, and to our relief came over in his vehicle which took about ten minutes.

"Shouldn't drive onto the sand in a car," he said in his Australian twang.

Pulling us out with a tow rope, we were back on terra firma. With no key, we had to make sure we didn't stop on the way back to Adelaide. And we were nearly late for curtain up!

You might say we were pretty stupid that day. We are human!

Apropos the people we stayed with in Adelaide. Years later, I was in the Albert Hall during a concert. In the interval, I wandered around the back. A woman rushed up to me, threw her arms around me and kissed me. She knew my name. So I felt I must know her from somewhere. But I hadn't a clue who she was. I let her talk... when she said "Adelaide..." oh goodness! We had stayed with them. It was their car that had sunk into the sand. I'm glad to report that she never guessed I hadn't recognised her. It had been a long time after all!!

You may be wondering when I write that we had a honeymoon. Where had Mary gone—Richard's first wife? She had been a casualty of a singer's life: too many absences, too many late nights, too many lonely evenings spent away. It is incredibly lonely without a companion.

No one's fault, just a profession that takes you away to the ends of the earth.

They had amicably split. Always friends and a son between them. I had a son too, Nigel... the two boys (now men) are close.

Our Wedding

We married on May 25th 1963. Not the usual format. No rushing away on a honeymoon. No disco into the night. That evening Richard sang *Fidelio*! Glyndebourne put all my relatives in boxes. The chorus (who had been our choir) were in a mellow mood. Florestan probably the happiest in its history!

That particular production of *Fidelio* was notable for the singer who sang the main part: Gré Brouwenstijn, a Dutch soprano. She was ideal: tall, statuesque, with a wonderful voice. In the dungeon scene when she finally finds her husband, it was the most moving I have ever heard.

Harold Rosenthal of *Opera Magazine* wrote that Richard was the finest Florestan he had heard. It is of course a dramatic tenor part, not a lyric tenor. But what Richard did with it was thrilling. I always thought it a shame that Covent Garden would never see him in the role in the bigger house. Certainly, on May 25th any inhibitions he might have had were absent!

Fidelio is a complex opera. It took Beethoven a long time to complete it. It had a very chequered career. For such a great composer, he found the opera format difficult, just as Schubert had. So the opera has weaknesses. On the other hand, it has great operatic characters: provides Leonore with one of the most difficult arias in opera and makes Florestan wait until the last scene to sing at all. Not so easy when his first note is a long sustained 'Gott' on top A. How you concede that when Florestan has been starved, he would have a healthy top A? On the other hand, the audience expects it to be a great note.

Richard Lewis and Gré Browenstijn in Fidelio by
Beethoven at Glyndebourne

Our Wedding Day

Chapter Eight
King Priam by Michael Tippett

This opera also took London by storm on the 29th of May 1962.

Tippett's first opera *Midsummer Marriage* with Richard and Joan Sutherland had not been successful. The singers were puzzled by the text. It seems that Tippett was too. And he wrote the libretto. It was too difficult and obscure. Rather convoluted. Esoteric.

Reviews:

"No British composer need break his heart if his work is not heard in England because, frankly, no impresario would even have considered it in the past at Covent Garden."

Colin Mason liked it: "Joan Sutherland and Richard Lewis were magnificent, dramatically and visually. It was an overwhelming experience."

It was Tippet's first opera. His second was a different story.

Terrific stage design by Sean Kenny. Sam Wanamaker produced. John Pritchard, the conductor. It would restore Tippett's reputation after the first opera had been viewed as too obscure and intellectual. Its strength was that most people knew the tale. The stage design was outstanding, and the artists chosen were ideal.

Forbes Robinson was a wonderfully powerful King Priam. It is a fiendishly difficult part, and Forbes was magnificent. Richard was a handsome Achilles with some of the best music. The scene between the two men, when Priam comes to beg for the body of his son Patroclus was intensely moving. Then the extraordinary war cry from Achilles sung in a rising lift, lights full on him as he rose, potent stuff indeed.

Tippett wrote an aria for Achilles set for guitar— extremely difficult, very evocative with an extraordinary guitar part. The guitarist was John Williams, then unknown.

"That player is fantastic," Richard told me. "He will go places!!"

Putting on the whole concept as Peter Hall saw it, with Pritchard conducting, was a towering spectacle. Nothing had been seen like it at Covent Garden before.

Reviews:

"British music was given a new meaning."

The Times wrote: "The Achilles of Richard Lewis, a part made in heaven for him, did full justice to the two landmarks in the opera. The song with guitar (played exquisitely by John Williams, then unknown) and the tremendous war cry in the second act, Achilles rising dressed in full armour which caught the spotlight, as he sang the bloodthirsty war cry."

The Times wrote: "It was a moment of theatrical history, more bloodcurdling than any schoolboy could imagine."

Martin Cooper wrote: "The great hopes aroused by his first opera have been more than fulfilled. Both Tippet's libretto and music reveal a new certainty and aim and unity of purpose as well as a mastery of musical language."

Max Loppert wrote: "How can opera be called infertile, barren. In Tippett's opera, there may be no stream of melody, but who, hearing the wonderful third act trio, can fail to sense a pent-up lyrical impulse, searching so movingly for fresh form and expression."

Michael Tippett was an interesting man. Tall and thin, rather handsome, quietly introvert and very intense. When I met him, he was concerned that his sight was going, which for a composer was pretty serious. He had a great affection for Richard. He once said to him, "I want you whenever I can. You are the only singer who makes my music sound natural."

Is his music still so esoteric? Or will it one day be heard with different ears?

Sir Michael Tippett with Richard Lewis after the World Premier of Tippett's King Priam at Covent Garden

More Glyndebourne
And Rake's Progress

There were, and are, so many wonderful productions at Glyndebourne. A book in itself, of which there are plenty. Initially, it was a Mozart House. Gradually, over the years, it moved into a broader repertoire.

Even Mozart can be overdone like a meal with no variety. You might think, "Gosh, nothing but Mozart, how wonderful." Not everyone did. Geoffrey Gilbertson, stage director at Glyndebourne once exclaimed when he heard the theatre was going to present other composers.

"Thank goodness. I've had enough Mozart to last my lifetime."

One notable opera was Stravinsky's *Rake's Progress*. It has had two productions.

But the one I know is with Richard. Producer Carl Ebert, Oliver Messel, the stage designer, Elsie Morison as Anne, David Ward, the father, Hugues Cuénod, the auctioneer. A classic production.

Richard had taken over the role. The American tenor originally booked was ill. Glyndebourne was not sure if Richard was right for the role, but there was no one else to take it over at such a short notice. So it was a great chance for him to move out of classical roles, find a new direction.

"I went for a holiday, and learned it sitting by the sea."

In three weeks.

As it turned out, it was a good move.

Moran Caplat, General Manager, would say, "We began to realise that we had a winner. Richard was made for the role."

They took it to Edinburgh first. The critics were good. The cast there was Elsie Morison as Anne Trulove, Hervey Alan as her father, Jerome Hines as Nick, plus Mary Jarred, Nan Merriman and Murray Dickie. Alfred Wallenstein conducted. (Paul Sacher conducted in 1954 at Glyndebourne but not in Edinburgh).

Of Richard, the critics wrote:

"His singing production and diction were in the best tradition of opera singing, and his acting could scarcely have been better."

"Here was excellent acting and characterisation, musical intelligence and robust singing of the first order. A magnificent performance!"

He had brought it off. Proved he could act, move into more versatility.

And not so many king roles. It is so easy to become typecast. He wanted better dramatic possibilities. It was a time when more realistic acting was asked for. Until then, it had often been 'one arm up, one arm down' technique. Singers were now expected to be able to not only sing but act. Today, this is taken for granted to make singing seem as if it is natural to stand and sing and express emotion. Maybe that is what Tippett saw in his singing. It isn't, of course, but we had to make it seem so. For so long, the voice came first. Now, it was the voice and the drama.

The Rake's Progress
At Glyndebourne

A slight change of cast. David Ward as the father, Hugues Cuénod as the auctioneer, David Ward, large impressive looking man, well over six foot. A proud Scot (he ended up living in a castle in Scotland) was a very nervous performer. It was said that he would fortify himself with a drink… not a good idea.

Gloria Lane, the American singer, sang Baba the Turk. An exotic, well-endowed, stunning woman. With a beard, moustache, and a low-cut dress showing off her dimensions, she made an attractive if unusual sight.

Richard sang a *Carmen* with Gloria at Covent Garden. Apart from a magnificent voice, and outgoing sexual physical Carmen necessities, she was not afraid to flaunt them. With one interesting moment when her bosom fell out in an act one duet.

I asked Richard:

"What did you do?"

"Tucked it back," answered our tenor!

Another interesting singer Tamara Chumakova sang the brothel Madam. She was a large red-headed Russian with a deep contralto voice. In the seduction scene, Richard would often find his head between the cliffs of her well-endowed bosom. She was actually a member of the chorus, but was so right for the brothel madam that Glyndebourne gave her the part.

Hugues Cuénod, the Swiss tenor, a tall lanky highly intelligent man who made a great career without a lot of voice.

By sheer intelligent singing he made a reputation all over the world. He sang his first role at the Metropolitan Opera when he was eighty!

He was the auctioneer which is a complex scene, testing the chorus as well as the soloist. Stravinsky conceived what was an extraordinary and effective operatic scene.

Critics seemed happy:

"Richard Lewis, a fine and dependable artist, sang his best as Tom Rakewell, and it is doubtful if any other British tenor could have sung this role so perfectly."

Dr Carl Ebert was the producer then. The mad scene at the end of the opera was a masterclass in producing. The Rake is in bedlam. This is a mad house. This great German actor could draw out singers, making them think through why and for what reason they were singing. A master in the inner workings of a role.

It is an odd opera. Full of melody. A surprise coming from Stravinsky. He provided great roles. Each act, each scene different, creating the characters which were taken from Hogarth's etchings of the *Rake's Progress*.

A strong part for baritone is the part of 'Nick' who is the devil. He gives Tom three riddles to solve, set in a graveyard, where he has a grave dug ready for Tom. Tom tricks him. Furious at losing his prey, Nick sends him mad as a last vengeful parting shot.

So Richard would mark down this production as a big move towards being recognised as an actor as well as a singer. He had come a long way from the smogs of Manchester, had risen above those five years lost in the war, had found a home at Glyndebourne where he worked with top musicians. He had started late. At thirty-two he had to make up for lost time in the spotlight of the London opera scene. Those five years in the army had maybe robbed him of opportunity, but in many ways, this would be to his advantage. His voice was fresh, and singing with orchestras in Brussels and Oslo had turned him into a reasonably experienced artist.

He was now recognised as a Mozartian... His versatility in style and voice was opening up opportunities. Not only dramatic singing (Mahler's *Das Lied von der Erde* for example, which he would record four times with Ormandy, Leinsdorf, Szell and Bruno Walter) but some of the standard opera roles (which although he felt were not his metier, they were bread and butter) such as *Madam Butterfly*, *Traviata*, *Der Freischütz* and *Carmen*, which he occasionally took on...

He knew that he was at his best in the lyric, baroque early romantic music. And that he had this reputation for assimilating modern scores.

Chapter Nine
Promenade Concerts

Every year the renowned Sir Henry Wood Promenade Concerts take place in the Albert Hall. (Now called the BBC Promenade Concerts) A very important one for performers from all over the world. Richard would be booked almost every year though his career.

One year, he was voted the most popular singer by the Promenaders.

Now that's an accolade not easily won. Promenaders are a special bunch of loyal, passionate music lovers, so you have to be very special to win their allegiance.

That year when they voted Richard Lewis as their favourite singer was a high compliment.

"Worth more than an Oscar," he said.

But you have to keep on your toes. For the prommers are mostly young, ardent students quick to criticise.

"When I sang Gerontius (from memory), if I made a small error, every prommer head would look up. They followed scores. Quite a test for a singer."

Since then, the concerts have had to adapt to a modern world. Young people have myriads of outlets for music. Popular music plays such a major part in life today. So the

'Proms' have embraced music that in Richard's day would have been astonishing. Then it was completely traditional. Of course, so was the profession. It was hidebound. People in charge were from a past generation. Most of the teaching staff in the schools of music were performers of long ago... not like today.

You can forget very quickly how stressful it can be to perform... a student singer needs someone who understands this., Looking back, teaching today is markedly better.

Things change, of course. And will change again. It has become all the more exciting and innovative. The young want something different, and if you don't change, you die.

Sir Malcolm Sargent (Flash Harry) always conducted the final promenade concert. He loved every minute. This dignified man, immaculately dressed in his tails, engulfed by toilet rolls that the prommers had thrown.

Another great conductor was...

Chapter Ten
Bruno Walter

Bruno Walter was a major figure in British music. Not long after the war, Richard had the opportunity to sing with him. He and Kathleen Ferrier were engaged to sing with Walter in Mahler's *Das Lied von der Erde*. After the performance, the plan was to record it with Decca, a huge chance for a relatively unknown singer.

Unfortunately, this very fact posed a problem. At that point in time, the recording company had not yet heard of Richard Lewis. So they brought in Julius Patzak, the Viennese tenor.

"I saw him walking in during rehearsal," Richard told me. "It was a big disappointment at the time."

However, he would sing with Walter many times.

Only recently, I have learned that a recording WAS made at a concert in Manchester. I have the CD. It is wonderful: Ferrier superb and Richard in his prime.

He sang many times with Kathleen Ferrier. This wonderful contralto had an ability to make everyone love her. She was a typical northern girl with a northern sense of humour.

She would not think twice of throwing her skirts up to show "me warm coms" as she called them. And you needed them in cathedrals, I can tell you.

Richard was singing with her in a *Messiah* not long before she died of cancer. He told me of the strength of her will, how she never felt sorry for herself.

In the world of singers, whoever comes to the top is remarkable. There are many good ones who never make it. How much does luck play? Today, there are colleges turning out hundreds of singers every year. There is only so much room. Yes, Richard had his share of luck. But he grabbed it with both hands. He had particular assets to sell such as his capacity to assimilate complex modern scores which was an ability to pitch notes against modern orchestration, not something he found difficult. Tippett would say, as would Walton, Luigi Nono, Stravinsky, Menotti:

"I only want Lewis."

So what is it conductors want? Reliability. The job is difficult enough. It might look easy watching a singer perform. It is an exercise in pure energy, that fusing of two minds with the same intent, the same musical journey like an unseen thread running between conductor and singer.

Maureen Forrester, the Canadian contralto, when she was asked by a student, "What is the secret of success?" she replied "Re-engagement, dear."

How true. If a conductor does not like you, or you come to rehearsal not knowing the work very well, you won't be asked back.

Chapter Eleven

Singers should be careful what they do. At the Edinburgh Festival, Richard was singing a work in which the tenor starts on the first page.

At rehearsal, he found his chair had a wobbly leg. He asked the stage staff to make sure it was changed before the evening. When he walked out in the evening, it was still there. In anger, he tore out the first page of the score, scrumpled it up and threw it on the floor. The orchestra began. He realised he had to start the work and had to bend down to retrieve it!

But conductors are human. I always knew when Sir Georg Solti had lost his way in a score. He would wave his arms fairly wildly until he had got back.

Many times, a conductor would look at a singer in an effort to find his way back.

Eugene Ormandy was a Hungarian who came to the USA as a violinist. He took over the Philadelphia Orchestra to build it up in to one of the finest in the USA. Concerts took place in the Concert Hall, which was famous for having superb acoustics. However, he had one little quirk. He had a disconcerting habit, much to his orchestra's consternation, of conducting a new work from memory. This can be dangerous and nerve-wracking for the artists. During a *Missa Solemnis* of Beethoven, conducting it for the first time without a score, he threw a wrong cue at Richard who ignored it.

I recall a *Mass* in B minor in Edinburgh. A well-known Russian soprano was singing with Carlo Maria Giulini (and Richard). She obviously didn't know it. Giulini (conducting) told her to go and find a room and learn it!

This conductor was much admired by Richard. He was a quiet, dedicated man with a strong concept of how to perform a great work, often asking that the singers perform it from memory. This does not always go down well with some singers. It's relatively easy (I qualify that with relatively!) to turn up and sing from the score. But have the singers explored the work in depth? What Giulini wanted was to present music that has been learned, so expression can be projected, not so easy with your head in the score. I remember well his Mozart *Requiem* in the Festival Hall: a revelation for the listener and for the performers.

Publicity

We have heard how Richard premiered Tippett's *Midsummer Marriage* with Joan Sutherland, also *King Priam* in Coventry at the Festival (the same Festival where Britten's *War Requiem* was premiered.) Two major British works, unprecedented at the time.

That was something to shout about. We certainly were amazed that here, in Britain, a country that could rarely boast the premier of a new work, had not just one, but two in the same week yes, we celebrated.

Would it be different today—with media outlets, pirated recordings, immediate international exposure, headlines. questions, of course, digging for anything that might be racial?

Britten's *War Requiem*, sung by a British singer (Peter Pears) and a German baritone (Fischer-Dieskau), would there be someone marching against this? Holocaust deniers.

Chapter Twelve
Pavarotti... Mario Lanza

A great tenor who was very good at self-promotion. A larger-than-life man who sold his product, if that's how it can be described. Promotion. And what greater promotion could there be than The Three Tenors, a phenomenon that endures to this day? Three wonderful singers exploiting the public avid for the excitement of popular arias sung by people who knew how to play on the need out in the public arena.

And exciting it was. Pavarotti doing his best to out sing Domingo, who in turn out sang Carreras.

That was part of the fun!

Luciano Pavarotti knew what he wanted and where he wanted to go.

We as a nation find this difficult. British artists were always reluctant to shout about what they do, the successes they had. The British nature? Reticent? Self-promotion looked down on. Things have totally changed.

For Richard, the ballyhoo of press interviews was torture. For Pavarotti, it was how he planned: the image, the flamboyance. While it would have been sensible for Richard to emulate Luciano, he could not. He was stubborn. Didn't see why if his voice was in demand, he had to publicise it.

His publicity person, Alex, was frustrated. She arranged a TV interview in New York. We arrived. Two hours later, we were still waiting to go on. By ten o'clock, Richard had had enough, so he left. The interviewer had to introduce an absent singer.

Another press exposure was a meeting with Mario Lanza in Hollywood. To Richard's surprise, when he was introduced in Lanza's dressing room the famous film tenor said, "How I envy you."

"Why, when you are known all over the world from your films?"

Lanza replied, "What I really want is to sing opera in an opera house. I auditioned at the Met, but they told me my voice was too small."

One can suppose, therefore, that when we hear a film such as *The Great Caruso* (I saw it four times when I was in my teens) the sound is turned up to make Lanza sound as if he had a big voice.

He came, at our invitation, to a performance at the opera, causing quite a sensation when he arrived! But whatever the Met said, Lanza gave millions of people pleasure. He became the tenor who made the world realise that singing was an emotional and hardworking profession.

Publicity? Now it is vital. Web, Facebook, Twitter—the more, the better. But in the forty years since the development of media coverage, when a happening is out there, this world has changed. You go with it or you die.

There are always drawbacks. Now, the soul of a singer is examined. Private life invaded. You have to agonise why you sing something. What does it mean? Characters that have been a mainstay of opera are now questioned. Was Butterfly treated in a racist way? Was Don Giovanni a rapist? Probably.

That would have appalled Pavarotti. And Richard too. In fact, anyone from their era would not have understood.

What sort of man was Pavarotti? Really nice, with a naive sincerity that was attractive. That he had a voice to die for (especially in his prime) was something he took for granted. He premiered in Britain at Glyndebourne with his first foray out of Italy taking the musical world by storm.

"Why would he sing at Glyndebourne?" I heard a man behind me in the audience say to friends. That is curious. I can only assume that because he became so big, a giant in terms of world exposure, that many people would presume he would not have appeared at the small Glyndebourne theatre. But didn't we all smile at his gimmicks? The handkerchief, the smiling larger-than-life man, that had not been developed when we knew him. That would come later, perhaps as the voice got older. For the music that such a tenor sings is hugely hard to maintain. The top Cs have to be maintained. When he could do it, I have never heard better.

He arrived aged 25, unknown, and created a sensation.

"A young tenor singing with me in *Idomeneo* is excellent," Richard told me. "He will go a long way."

However, Luciano did not take to the Glyndebourne discipline. Used to the looser, less-disciplined world of Italian opera, he had a job settling down. One big problem was that there was no prompt box for him to depend on, an Italian singer's necessary prop. But Luciano did learn his role and sang it without a prompt. And he was very good.

But I don't think that he was comfortable.

Later, Richard and he were booked to sing *Idomeneo* in Geneva straight after the Glyndebourne season. Was Pavarotti, fresh from Glyndebourne without his prompt, able to dispense with the Geneva prompt? Not a bit of it. It was as if it had never happened. Back he went to his dependency and, personally, I think he was better without it. Somewhat like a singer who sings with a score. It is always better without... Communication, that's the business we are in!

He had a nice sense of rational thinking though, as proved in an interview with Terry Wogan who asked him two questions.

One was, "What might you have been if you hadn't been a singer?"

His answer was "Maybe a garbage collector... but I would have been the best garbage collector in the country."

Another question was, "What's it like to be the most famous singer in the world?"

His answer, "There are others out there just as good, but I'm the one who's here," he answered.

That seems a very fair response.

Richard Lewis with Mario Lanza

Luciano Pavarotti (third from left) and Richard Lewis in
Mozart's Idomeneo at Glyndebourne

The Prompt Box

If the reader has never seen a prompt box or maybe doesn't know there is one, let me give you an idea. It is set in the well of the stage right at the feet of performers. In it, a prompter will sit dispensing cues to the singer... shouting, singing, gesticulating. You might ask what's the point of the conductor then? Well, he is the director of the whole package, but that's how it's done in Italy.

Italian singers are brought up on this comfort fall back. British singers, never. There's nothing to crow about. It's just a different way of doing things. Remember that the whole art form of opera began in Italy. It was the Italians who set the early rules.

Luciano Pavarotti was the most recent tenor who followed an Italian tradition of great tenors: Caruso, Gigli, Martinelli,

A warm-hearted great singer. Who has not thrilled to his *Nessun Dorma?*. But I believe he never understood the different operatic cultures. And it might surprise you to know that he did not read music too well. Did that deter him? Of course not. He had superb coaches and répétiteurs.

I believe Frank Sinatra did not read music, and I guess he went a long way!

A répétiteur is a pianist who will coach a singer in his or her role.

Luciano, at the end of that Glyndebourne season, asked us to spend Christmas with him and his family. We were unable to. I would have loved to. I asked him what Christmas was like in Italy and in his home.

"We cooka forr fourr days… we eata forr fourrr days," was the reply.

While it would have been interesting to join him and his family, that much eating?

A little story. During the Glyndebourne *Idomeneo* when the duet between Idomeneo and Idamante comes (the point after Idomeneo has made a vow to the gods to sacrifice the first person he meets on the shore… and of course, it is his son). The duet is poignant. In some performances, Richard was affected by the emotion through the music, which Pavarotti later said he didn't understand. (He was only 28) Many years later, he would say in an interview that, "I did not understand why Lewis was weeping… now I do, for I have children, and I would be moved too."

I will tell you a story that shows how singers think. One afternoon, I was in the Glyndebourne car with a young tenor. I found out he was understudying Richard in *Idomeneo*.

"No chance of doing it. Lewis is never ill… anyway it's an easy role, I could do it without any problem."

I said nothing. But that evening before the pre-dress rehearsal, Richard mentioned he had a bit of a throat, I asked him why didn't he let his understudy take the rehearsal. He decided to. The next day, I went back stage to listen. The understudy sang very well. But when he came off stage, he saw me. "That was harder than I realised," he said, sweat pouring off him.

Of course, it is!

The Claque

Every Italian opera house has a 'claque'—someone who is paid to clap, cheer, or even boo if paid—which brings to mind an incident in San Francisco.

Richard was singing Don Jose in *Carmen*. There came a knock at his dressing room door. Opening it, a small Italian-looking man stood there, "Meester Lewis, I am the resident claque. I must tell you will not get a clap or cheer when you sing your big aria if you sing the high B pianissimo," he said. "I can make sure you do."

"Thank you, but no."

"Ah, signore, you will have a bad audience reaction to this," and he left.

The aria has a final top B in pianissimo which Bizet asks for. Most tenors belt it out, which is much easier than pianissimo. Richard sang it as written. He didn't need a claque!

It occurred to me later that the 'resident claque' might have started booing!!

As I write, I remember things.

Sir John Barbirolli, who was of Italian origin, wanted to record Puccini's *Love Duets*. He asked for Richard and an American soprano Leonora Lafayette. Why Richard when there were plenty of Italian tenors perhaps more suited to the genre of Italian music? Reason? He wanted the Puccini to be sung keeping to the composer's dynamic marking (who was always specific. If he put pppp he meant very soft). This recording was so successful it was in the market for years. And can still be bought today. On it, Richard proved that he had the passion and 'welly' to interpret Puccini.

Which brings me to a wonderful *Don Giovanni in San Francisco*. I write wonderful because I have never seen or heard a better cast than that one.

Singers were Elisabeth Schwarzkopf (Donna Elvira), Victoria De Los Ángeles (Donna Anna), Geraint Evans (Leporello), Cesare Siepi (Don Giovanni), Richard (Don Ottavio) and Reri Grist (Zerlina).

Two prima donnas in one production! Problems? Schwarzkopf, very much the Prima primadonna. De Los Ángeles, very much the feminine woman. She had only just recovered from a miscarriage so was vocally fragile. Coming to her big and difficult aria *Non mi dir* she implored Richard to stay by her side and hold her.

As she sang, I saw Schwarzkopf standing the other side of the stage, just hidden by the curtain from the audience. She did nothing. Just standing there was enough to disturb De Los Ángeles.

One evening as Schwarzkopf walked around the stage singing, in a music break, she saw me standing. "Darling," she called, "I am dying for a pee." Honestly. True. Could I forget such a thing?

Geraint Evans came across a problem with Schwarzkopf too. In his letter aria *Madamina* in which he describes the conquests of Don Giovanni, Schwarzkopf, all the way through, made gestures designed to take attention away from Geraint. I won't print his expletives(in Welsh!). He wasn't having it. The next performance, he sang it upstage, which made Schwarzkopf have her back to the audience. There was nothing she could do about it.

If all this sounds like backstage gossip, I suppose it is. But I found it fascinating.

One last thing about Schwarzkopf, a soprano that I admire hugely. Was there ever a better Marschallin in *Der Rosenkavalier* or Strauss's *Four Last Songs*?

Elisabeth was a great beauty and, on stage, a powerful and attractive sight.

She was married to Walter Legge who recorded for EMI, producing many now famous recordings, not least with his wife. But he was a Germanic-styled rigid man, and many a row occurred when a recording was taking place.

Elisabeth had a certain reputation from the Second World War that would follow her. During the war, it was said she fraternised with German officers, so when it ended, she had to explain. Stories followed her as they do.

If I tell stories that don't reflect well on someone, well, it's a time of great people who were not perfect. It's not a 'kiss and tell'. I just say it as I saw it.

Stories abound in this profession. So believe this if you want.

Elisabeth was on a plane going somewhere. She sat with a colleague. Her husband had just died.

He said, "So sorry to hear about Walter, Elisabeth, you must miss him."

"Ah, no," she cried, "he is always with me."

"I'm sure he is," he answered.

"No, no… I mean it. Here is my Walter," pulling out a box. In it were Walter's ashes!

I mentioned Geraint Evans earlier, a close friend of Richards. They were in San Francisco together in the early days. Of all the singers that I came across, none had the stage charisma of Geraint. He had the looks of a gypsy which fitted well with many operatic roles, not least Papageno or Figaro or Leporello. I can honestly say I never heard any singer sing and act these characters as well as he did—a totally classic stage animal. He was also a charmer, which I will leave and just say that he loved women.

Chapter Thirteen
Puerto Rico... Pablo Casals

Now that was a booking to remember! The great Casals. WHY he was in Puerto Rico, I never knew. Had he left Spain all together? Had he any regrets? This great cellist exiled from Spain for his beliefs, never to play again. There we were in the balmy climate of Puerto Rico, classical music clashing incongruously with its surroundings, adulation of everyone around Casals, the man who sacrificed his playing for an ideal. What an aura of worship this man inspired!

Was he right to stop playing for a moral reason—the greatest cellist of his time? And did it stop the ugly things in the world?

We certainly had a wonderful time in the Festival. The long flight was worth it as we walked into that balmy air, tropical palms waving in the black starry sky, swimming in a sea so warm it was almost like a sauna. So speaks someone used to the icy water of Scotland.

Clifford Curzon, the great British pianist, had the job of accompanying Richard in a recital. Remember, this was a solo pianist, one of the greats, but alas, no accompanist.

Singers must have a pianist who gives, listens, communicates. Curzon did none of these. He gave nothing.

Certainly, did not listen. And communication was totally absent. It ended up a solo piano recital with our tenor doing his best to keep up.

Casals sat backstage listening. "Richard is a very great artist," he whispered to me.

He was a diminutive figure, very old by then. I would like to have spent time with him. But he rarely mixed with the artists. He had a very young wife. She had been his student. At the age of, I think, about eighty-five, he had the good fortune to have a twenty-something-old partner, beautiful, dark haired, caring for this great man with loving devotion.

Talking about accompanists, I once asked that great accompanist Geoffrey Parsons why he didn't play solo as well as accompanying. He had just sat down at our piano and knocked off a Mozart sonata beautifully.

"It's two quite different art forms," he replied. "Being a soloist is not to how I see what I do. I am not a protagonist; I am a supporter. To me, playing for a great singer or instrumentalist is what I have been designed for, not the battlefield of concerto playing."

I truly believe that Geoffrey knew what you were going to do before you did it, which gives great comfort in the difficult world of recital singing.

He accompanied Richard on an Australian concert tour. Together for many weeks, they became great friends.

Geoffrey Parsons and Richard Lewis

Geoffrey Parsons and Richard Lewis in Recital at
Beverley Minster

At recital in Sydney, the organisers had rubbed a substance on the piano to make it look good for the TV cameras. What they hadn't realised was that it would come off on the singer's jacket. When Richard turned to walk off, all his jacket and trousers were covered in white.

Chapter Fourteen
Vienna

There is a system, if that's what you call it, of the profession's biggest singers doing what is called the opera circuit. A singer is booked for a role they have a reputation for. They do not rehearse. They arrive, sing that evening, then leave the next morning for another opera house.

While this swells the bank accounts, it is not in the interests of good opera. I have heard tales of a singer who only met her fellow performer on the stage.

Such a system is prevalent in Vienna, a system that Richard became involved in when he arrived to sing. He had been engaged to sing in *Don Giovanni* and *The Magic Flute*.

He arrived, and as was his habit, rang the music director to see when his rehearsals were.

"We do not have rehearsals, Mr Lewis."

"Well, can I have a music rehearsal with the conductor?"

"This we do not do."

"Well, unless I get a rehearsal, I will not be singing," was his response.

He got a music rehearsal, nothing more. The first time he met the cast of *Don Giovanni* was on stage. All he could do with no stage direction was to follow what he had done before.

A difficult moment came when he had sung *Dalla Sua Pace*, the first aria for Don Ottavio. The safety curtain came down behind him as he was singing. Finishing the aria, he looked for the exit. Tried one side, no luck. Tried the prompt side... again no luck. Kept coming back to bow. By now, he had had two ovations. Someone shouted to him from the wings, which he could not hear or understand. Then the conductor (during a third bow) pointed downwards. His exit was down through the orchestra!

"Someone might have told me."

He goes down in history as the only tenor who had three ovations for one aria...

A strange way of putting on opera, dodgy too. Anyone with little experience would and could find themselves in trouble. But this international system is used in some (not all) houses. Plenty of money to be made that way but artistically sterile.

If you compare the intense rehearsals at Glyndebourne with the system in Vienna (and some other European houses), you can see why performances in the Sussex house are so unique.

The world of singing and, in particular, opera is a strange one. Performers become nomads, rootless, called to fly the globe wherever they are wanted.

Possibly today even more so. The planet has become smaller and smaller.

Opera takes place in most countries. And they want singers. Singers don't carry their voices in a bag ready to be taken out or changed if not working properly. You are stuck with it for life. A delicate instrument at the mercy of the elements: sitting in planes with air conditioning, hotels, where the windows won't open, different climates. One month in the tropics, the next in sub-zero temperatures. Long rehearsals, nowhere to practise.

And friends. You make firm and lovely relationships while rehearsing and performing. But the end comes, time to say goodbye. "Hope to see you again… try and write or email." But you never do. Another opera house, new friends. Just for a while.

Sometimes a booking can be in exotic places. When a singer can take time off to explore? Not often. There is 'the voice' to think of.

Which makes me think of a very exotic place when we went to the Argentine.

The theatre is the Teatro Colón in the centre of the busy city, which when we were there, looked like a building site: the roads and pavements piles of rubble, waiting to be mended. And the smells! Mixtures of food emanating from the many restaurants mixed with the rubbish littering the streets. The theatre was old: cockroaches and fleas abounded. Curtain up, approximate. Pay was irregular dependant on the rate of exchange. Singers would queue up outside the Bureau de Change to see what their fee was worth that day.

But like all old theatres, it had a distinguished history. Most great singers from the past and the present had sung there.

We had two weeks between performances, so decided to go and see some of the Argentinian country. The British Embassy organised it. They couldn't have chosen a more out-of-the-way place.

It was called Jujuy. Deep into the interior, we flew in a four-seater plane, the only way to get to this remote place.

After a day sightseeing, we left by car driving into a wild, majestic country. The mountains and forests seemed to be untouched by civilisation. The only people we saw were Indians, who had never seen (it seemed to me) anyone European and certainly not a tall blonde (if the reaction to myself was anything to go by!!) I never saw anyone but Indians when we were there. No tourists, no people with camera, except us, of course. It was the women who interested me the most. They wore men's hats. They were the ones who did all the work. The men gathered round fires or sat at tables drinking while their women toiled.

We drove further and further into the mountains, attended a religious festival attended by huge crowds of worshippers. As in many Catholic countries, the church plays a vital part of human life. Here it was no exception. We were caught up in the procession which was a parade with the Virgin Mary carried on a litter above us on a platform going into the church.

I watched them walking on their knees: woman with babies at their breast, some had padding on their knees to help them as they shuffled towards the church doors. Then queuing to get into the church where there was incense and gold and silver, entering the church door where the priests in their gold and silver vestments waited for them—perhaps the only beauty they knew in their poverty.

Then later, we went to a festival where food was cooked by brightly dressed women. I had noticed that the men sat around smoking while the women worked.

"Don't refuse any food," the Embassy guide told us. "They would be offended."

I would have preferred not to, but actually what they gave us was delicious.

As we left, Richard sang to a group of Indians sitting round a fire in the dark night. They did not know who he was or where he came from. The guide told them he was from the opera house. It meant nothing.

Did he go down in their history?

"The day a stranger from another world sang to us."

Travelling

Richard was now in demand all over the world. We were touring for months at a time. By the time one has packed and unpacked suitcases for weeks on end, taken long plane journeys, life becomes endless travelling.

When something comes along that is an unmitigated joy, it makes it all worth it.

For quite a long time, Richard had been asked by a music teacher in a school (I forget where now) to sing for them in Bach's *St Matthew Passion* in a local church. The fee he was offered was not much, and Richard had no time to do it anyway. "Find a fee for me, and I'll do it," were his last words… By the end of the next year, the music teacher wrote to say that the fee had been raised, and would he now consider it?

Before I go on, do you sigh and think, "Why couldn't he just do it for nothing?"

I say it's his job, his living. You wouldn't ask a dentist to do your teeth for nothing. Or your son's teacher to teach him for nothing, but many people do think that if you have a voice, you should sing, if asked, at a party out in the street or after dinner. That often happens.

When a famous violist was asked to dine in New York, the hostess wrote, "And do bring your violin as well." He replied, "Madam, my violin does not dine out." (I think it was Fritz Kreisler.)

That's the same Kreisler who, seeing a fish shop with fish heads staring out at him, remarked:

"Ah, I remember, I have a concert tonight!"

So you want to know what happened when Richard decided to sing the *St Matthew* for this school? It was just amazing. Why? Because it was just one of those occasions when fame and money no longer mattered. It was pure music-making among lovely people, people who perhaps were amazed that such a famous singer would do it. And that he gave as much for them as if it had been the Albert Hall. I myself joined the choir and enjoyed a jolly good sing!

Igor Stravinsky

One day in the sixties, Stravinsky sent a message that he wanted to meet Richard. This was no formal meeting. It was just us and the composer in his garden in Los Angeles.

We were there for the San Francisco Opera at that time. We flew to Los Angeles to meet the great composer.

Igor Stravinsky had engaged Richard for his work *Persephone* and wanted to write something especially for him. This would turn out to be *Canticum Sacrum* for tenor and baritone to be performed at the Venice Festival.

Do I remember what we talked about? Yes, vividly. The composer: a vital quixotic man, not very tall, very intense eyes.

We sat in his garden. How I longed to ask him questions, such as why did he live in Los Angeles. It seemed to me to be an odd place for such a man. My poetic imagination felt he should be in Paris where the great Ballets Russes was born.

He put on an apron and cooked a spaghetti. Yes, I ate spaghetti cooked by one of the world's greatest composers, sitting in his garden, the birds singing, yet in the distance the sound of traffic roaring past.

Photograph of Igor Stravinsky, taken in his garden, in Los Angeles
by Richard Lewis

I had to ask about Diaghilev and the Ballets Russes.

Who could know better? This man who was in the centre of this extraordinary dance company in Paris who composed *The Firebird*, *The Rite of Spring*.

His eyes lit up when I mentioned it, "Ah, such wonderful people... Nijinsky... what a dancer. Difficult, yes, but on the stage!! Exciting times... my *Firebird*, yes, my dear, it was a time of a group of people, the like of whom will never be seen again."

I asked him about Diaghilev. "A strong man, dominating, bursting with ideas. Difficult, yes, but a man with such a passion."

Diaghilev: Russian art critic, patron, ballet impresario, and founder of the Ballets Russes. He presented Russian music in Paris (Boris Godunov with Chaliapin), used dancers Nijinsky and Pavlova.

The two men talked of a new work, Stravinsky wanting to dedicate it to Richard. This would be for the Venice Festival. And there lies a story...

The composer was notoriously tight with money. Earlier, he had composed his *Rake's Progress* for the Festival the previous year. It was a huge success. So the Festival asked him if he would compose something for the following year. He had received a very large fee for the Rake...

And of course, asked a similar fee for the next year's festival. It was agreed. They expected a work as long as the *Rake's Progress*. What they got was eighteen minutes, and by the time they realised, it was too late to do anything about it.

They had no choice but to pay him.

It was so short, it had to be performed twice. Once before the interval, and again, after Stravinsky conducted, Richard and Gérard Souzay sang. It took place in St Mark's Cathedral.

Evidently, a bit chaotic on the night. A first performance of a work by Stravinsky aroused huge publicity, there and all over the world. So Venice was packed, St Marks full to the rafters.

"As we walked in, a flash bulb exploded very near us. And the crush in the cathedral was huge," Richard told me.

He would sing in Venice many times. Once for Mahler's *Das Lied von der Erde* in the Doges palace. That was in the days when Venice had not yet been overwhelmed with tourism. We were treated like royalty, had a personal black and gold gondola. Kirstin Meyer, the Swedish mezzo soprano was the other soloist. The singers were paid their fees in lire. And they were good fees. With nowhere to put them, Richard gave me the money to look after. The lire were large then (before the Euro). I just about crammed them into my evening bag.

On another visit, not a singing visit, just a holiday, we decided to take a gondola just for two, to take us round the city. The gondolier was a little man with a big moustache, very jolly. Told us about various places as he took us round the inlets.

"Here where Mozart stayed," or… "Here Vivaldi lived."

And he was interested to learn we were English.

"I marry Scots girl."

He had met her when he stayed in Scotland selling ice cream.

"I take you to meet," he grinned… going down a small alley off the main waterway. He punted into a square filled with gondolas.

"Maria," he called. A buxom woman in an apron came running out, "Och Giovanni, you shouldna be doing this," in broad Scots.

In the winter when the city is empty, many of the gondoliers go over to Britain to sell their famous Italian ice cream. Giovanni had met his wife in Glasgow.

Israel

Wonderful land. The love of music. Where you feel the story of the Bible so strongly.

One year we were there when Daniel Barenboim was conducting the orchestra. He and Jacqueline du Pré were to be married. Jacqueline had gone through the rituals that all brides have to go through. When we got there, the nuptials were about to start.

Jacqueline had converted to Judaism. It was the joining of two extraordinary musicians, which would create great music for many years, until the tragedy of Jacqueline's terrible disease brought it to an end. What vital people these two great artists were. Starting married life with such hope.

We were there because Richard was singing with Barbirolli. And I must tell you this story…

After a rehearsal one afternoon, Sir John came out of the auditorium into the strong sunlight. He was tired. He thought it would be nice just to sit down on the steps for a moment, threw his hat down and dropped off to sleep with his back against the wall. When he woke up, there was twenty pounds in his hat!

In Los Angeles, we were dining in an exotic restaurant called Trader Vicks a Polynesian eating place. Janet Baker, Evelyn Barbirolli and Sir John were with us. On the menu, exotic drinks and a menu that evoked the south seas with its choice of mouth-watering food... Sir John cast his eye over it, then asked the waiter for "poached eggs on toast" who never batted an eyelid.

Back to Israel...

Later on, Richard was invited to give a series of recitals there. The first ones were in the lovely auditorium donated by wealthy American Jews.

The last one was in a cave.

The usual temperature there can be anything up to 80 degrees and humid... In a cave, humidity is extra high. So high that a piano has to be tuned several times during a concert. The poor singer? In dinner suit and bow tie, sweat rolled off him. And in such heat and humidity, it was like singing into cotton wool.

But whatever the drawbacks, and there are always some, what a country!

Leonard Bernstein and Others

In our business of making music, there are some who rise up to become pioneers, personalities, who are so talented that words can hardly describe them. Such a one was Leonard Bernstein.

Richard considered him to be one of the finest conductors he ever worked with. He recorded his *Spring Symphony* in New York.

I hear you asking who are others who fit the description above? Personally, I would put Daniel Barenboim in my list. No doubt many others, but there must be something special. Barenboim, for me, is high on the list. Great pianist, great conductor, but above all, the humanity that he gives to his work for me qualifies him for my regard.

New York, New York... Isn't there a Sinatra song called that? What a city! Teeming with life. Tough, yes. So ethnically mixed that you could meet every nationality in the street. An exciting country to sing in... Concert halls, opera houses, art galleries... so much energy.

For Richard, and for many singers, New York was a goal to reach: to appear in any of the great halls Carnegie Hall, Lincoln Centre.

It is often asked why he never sang with the Metropolitan Opera. Earlier, I talked about luck... the right place at the right time. Let me tell you. Early in his career, he had the opportunity to sing to them arranged by his agent. Unfortunately, the director was Rudolf Bing, who had been artistic director of Glyndebourne in the days after the war. Richard had never got on with him. So he came to New York, sang to the Metropolitan people and was turned down. Ironically, at the end of Richard's career, he was asked by the then director, Joan Ingpen, to sing in Britten's *Billy Budd*. That would have been a great end to his career.

Unfortunately, he had just signed up to sing it in San Francisco.

Peter Pears was engaged. In one week, *Billy Budd* was heard, sung by two British tenors either end of America!

In one unprecedented year, he sang three times in the Lincoln Centre in just one week! with Bruno Walter, Eugene Ormandy and George Szell.

One year, New York had energy problems which meant that everyone had to share taxis when they arrived. After we flew in, we found a cab, then just as we set off, the door opened and Gene Kelly got in. "Can I share?" he asked. Of course, he could. We had a great time.

Then, reaching downtown New York, Kelly said goodbye, and disappeared! He owes us twenty dollars! I heard many years later that he was well known to be tight with money. I forgive him. He was a great dancer!

After Richard died, I was invited to New York to join a celebration of Lenny Bernstein's life and work taking place in the Lincoln Centre. I was at a table with the leader of the New York Symphony, Stravinsky's close friend, Robert Craft, and other prominent people important to Bernstein. What was so obvious was what Bernstein had meant to all these people. His loss was felt in so many ways, a meteor that had inspired and energised a whole profession.

I was asked to give a speech. Can't remember a thing about it!

Bach Aria Group

This group was formed to tour America performing the cantatas of Johann Sebastian Bach.

The founder was a millionaire called William Scheide, a distinguished Bach scholar, who made it his mission to let people hear these extraordinary works.

The group has always been made up of four singers and four instrumentalists. Bill Scheide (as he was known) travelled with the group on tour. His knowledge of every cantata (and there are over two hundred) was phenomenal.

Travelling with Scheide was an experience. When on the road (and I know this as he was often in our car when touring), he saw a highway sign saying maybe 'Route 56', Bill would start singing and quote which cantata it came from.

It was a good group to work with. Very well paid, and superbly organised. Richard was asked (taking over from Jan Peerce). Maureen Forrester, Lois Marshall, Norman Farrow were the other singers. Instrumentalists Bernard Greenhouse, Samuel Baron, Robert Bloom, Pauln Ulanowsky were the ensemble. They toured America and Europe.

One summer, we all went to Dubrovnik in Yugoslavia, a beautiful town with its myriads of fascinating roofs and ancient buildings. We stayed in what was a small palace. I heard later that it had been the house where a middle-eastern millionaire had lived. With its baths lined with mosaic and gold leaf, and bedrooms that would have been at home in a brothel, it made for an interesting stay! Our views from the window were superb. The concerts were in a hall off one of the main alleys. Rehearsals took place in a sunlit room, overlooking the bay.

Might Johann Sebastian Bach seem a strange composer to hear in a town like Dubrovnik? The Germanic rather austere music more suited to the misty cold northern climes? Evidently, the Dubrovnik people did not think so. The concerts were packed out every night.

Paris

Richard was involved in two productions in Paris.

Moses and Aaron with Georg Solti. Later Strauss's *Elektra* with Birgit Nilsson singing Elektra. I had never heard this wonderful soprano close up. It was my first look at a dramatic soprano in action. Having mostly lived and worked with lyric voices in the baroque or early classical music, and even though I knew the music of Richard Strauss, hearing a soprano such as Nilsson in action maybe only three feet from where I was standing, was an experience.

So, what is different? A lot, in fact. Watching Nilsson was astonishing. A strong body, magnificent breathing, riding effortlessly above the huge orchestra, singing effort hidden by technique. And I mean effort. Relentless singing against an orchestral dynamic that no light soprano could compete with.

This may seem an odd thing to say. Maybe you have to be a singer to understand.

I watched from the wings each night, intrigued to see the huge physical power necessary to perform this heavy music.

You might ask, "Don't lyric voices have to do that too?" Of course. But singing is a very athletic and physically demanding art. With dramatic singing (Verdi, Wagner, etc.), the effort is greater. The orchestra in heavier, louder, more vocal pressure required. More singers have lost their voices singing Wagner, than any other.

The role that Richard sang was, Aegisthus Elektra's husband and mother's lover. He comes in at the end. Popular with singers. Why? Because he was paid as much for that small role as he was for the major role of Aaron in *Moses and Aaron*.

One night, there was a crisis. French farmers had gone on strike, pouring milk into the streets in protest. As we walked to the theatre for the performance, we could see milk running down the streets. A passive revolt, they seemed harmless enough.

The opera started and all was fine until the final act, when Aegisthus comes with dialogue in German: "Lichte, lichte. Ist neimand hier zu leuchten?" (Lights, lights, is no one here to light them?)

Just as he was about to start, stage and auditorium lights went out. An announcement was made. The audience evacuated, orchestra and soloists alike. It was a bomb scare. After about half an hour, the opera was resumed where it left off. The audience came back.

I don't need to tell you, and you are probably guessing, that the continuation caused some laughter when Richard called, "Is no one here to light us?"

The way the Paris Opera do things takes a bit of getting used to. For some reason, the tenor dressing room is so far away from the main area, that to hear the stage tannoy telling you it's time to go on was impossible. I had the job of listening at the end of the corridor.

Another odd thing they do: they pay the singers just before the performance, counting out the money in front of whoever might be there. No artist wants the whole world to see what they are earning. So every performance was a pantomime of singer trying to hide from curious eyes the money being counted out!

But Paris is Paris. History in the very sticks and stones. The roll call of great singers and dancers who have performed there endless. The tenor dressing room which would have had every great singer of the past sitting in the same seat as Richard.

And when you are not performing, there is Paris to see: meals in those sidewalk cafes, floating down the Seine the Bateau Mouche—a romantic city.

Preserving the Voice

The singing voice can be a burden. It is a responsibility. To look after it. When to say no. One year, Bayreuth contacted Richard:

"Would he sing *Lohengrin*?"

He replied, "Would love to, but it's too heavy for me."

"We'll keep the orchestra down," was the reply.

"No sorry, I want to go on singing Bach and Handel."

Probably right. Keeping the orchestra down was not an option. In the end, he would be competing with it. The voice would not thank him for that.

Paris Concert

We went to Paris for the Festival.

Richard had formed his own Bach Group when he returned from America. We had some great players with us: Oscar Schumsky, Neil Black, William Bennett, Leonard Cohen and Harold Lester. It was a superb ensemble. We performed mostly Bach, occasionally other Baroque composers. For a London concert, Edwin Roxborough composed a work for us.

In the Paris festival, the group had been booked to sing in a lovely church.

We arrived to rehearse. The door was locked. After a lot of banging on doors and phone calls, it was finally opened up by a reluctant caretaker. When we got in, the harpsichord was not only needing to be tuned, but was not even up on the platform. Harold managed to lift it and give it a quick tune. By now, we only had a short time to rehearse. The performance would begin at 6:30 pm. People began coming in. Soon it was packed.

Now, a problem arose. Richard had been warned that unless he got the fee that evening, they would never be paid. And he had the group to pay. He asked if they would pay it before the concert started. They refused. So he said, in that case, he would not sing. We all went on. As I walked into the church, I could hear his voice loud and clear: "If we do not get paid, I will not sing."

To compound this, the stands for the players kept collapsing! And they say performing is always a pleasure!

Finally, they relented.

My memory of a concert in Paris! Was it fun? Not really.

Is it only in retrospect that we remember performances and think they were pleasurable? Forgetting things that go wrong? Like school? "Yes, I enjoyed school," only to recall that you didn't at all.

Yes, I enjoyed that performance, you say, forgetting the small frustrations, that you felt sick or had a sore back. But like childbirth, you keep on doing it, forgetting the pain, remembering the joy.

Chapter Fifteen
Face the Music

Remember that panel game with Joseph Cooper, Richard Baker, Robin Ray, Joyce Grenfell, Valerie Solti? The silent piano? How we all tried to guess before the experts.

Every week, a celebrity musician would take part. The guests were well primed beforehand. Nobody wanted a well-known artist to be shown up.

So hints were dropped. The musician could go back home and think about an answer. It was a wonderful game show. Not just for music lovers or musicians. The whole country was involved. What did Joseph play on the dummy piano?

During Ascot week, he and Richard were invited to join the Royal family at Windsor Castle to entertain them after dinner.

This meant we would be dining with the Royal Party, Richard singing to them after dinner, accompanied by Cooper. Wives were invited too.

We arrived, to be told that the Royal Party would greet us. In walked the Queen, Princess Margaret, The Duke of Edinburgh, Lord Snowdon, The Queen Mother, The Shah of Persia and his wife. Told not to ask the Queen a question, I'm afraid I did. Don't know what came over me really, for I said:

"In your many palaces are there parcels or boxes still waiting to be opened?"

The Queen laughed, "Oh, yes, indeed. There are unopened boxes from the time of Henry VIII still waiting."

Now that I couldn't believe! Fascinating!

The Shah seemed very autocratic, quite frightening. Actually, Prince Charles assured me that he rarely met commoners, and one could lose a head if not careful! I think he was having me on!

Prince Charles took me in to dinner. Richard took Princess Margaret who assured him she couldn't stand opera and smoked non-stop right through the meal.

Richard met again the photographer who had often been at Glyndebourne and was married to the Princess, Tony Armstrong-Jones, not a happy man.

"God, I'd do anything to get out of this bloody place," were his exact words. Well, he did.

We ate from silver plates. Told by Prince Charles that as this was an informal event, only the silver ones were used! On formal events, the guests ate from gold plates. Now that would have been nice. I tried not to feel short changed!

Prince Charles was scintillating and charming and very curious. He was around twenty-five, I think. Conversation was easy. One thing, however, posed a small problem. The meat was gristly. Oh, dear! Not easy to complain especially to the heir to the throne.

So what to do?

Spit it out? Swallow it? I swallowed it.

There is an etiquette to dining with the Queen. If she turns to her left, everyone follows. No one told me about that. So I went on chatting happily to Prince Charles, until he gave me the hint that I must talk to the Duke of Kent on my left.

Oh, dear, had I made a faux pas!

After the dessert, the doors were flung open. A lone piper came in. If that didn't make a magical end to my evening!

"Mother is woken every morning by her piper," Prince Charles told me.

Now that sounds perfect.

Entertaining the Royal party after dinner, Richard and Joseph had chosen some fairly serious songs. Probably light songs would have been better. But everyone seemed to enjoy them.

I sat behind the Duke of Edinburgh. He was not enjoying it. He read a newspaper throughout the recital. I hadn't the nerve to interrupt him, but I would like to have asked him about San Francisco.

He had been entertained by a British woman we knew the month before we had been there, in her beautiful flat overlooking The Golden Gate Bridge.

San Francisco Opera has a large group of women who are supporters, mostly widows, very wealthy. They have boxes at the opera and do a lot of fundraising for the company. It is a social affair mixed with intense fundraising.

The person we knew was a British woman, Margaret St Aubyn who had married a very wealthy American. She invited me to tea one afternoon. I then had a son who had just learned to walk. I think she soon regretted it.

In this exquisite apartment, he tottered about, all around him tables loaded with porcelain and glass. I could see my hostess getting worried. I left fairly speedily. She did not argue.

Aberdeen House

If you like tales of mixing with aristocracy, in particular, in Scotland, land of the pipes, the kilt, and Haggis, I can tell you of a visit to Aberdeen House.

Richard was invited by Lady Aberdeen to sing *Dream of Gerontius* in her home, a castle outside Aberdeen. Janet Baker had also been asked, and I think John Shirley Quirk.

Lady Aberdeen, a very competent conductor (studied, I believe, with Malcolm Sargent) put on regular concerts in her home where a special hall had been built. Aberdeen House was a castle with all the ingredients we imagine: a craggy magnificent pile, with magnificent high-ceilinged rooms crammed with lovely furniture, even a coal scuttle with inlaid wood to match the furniture in the main room. The ultimate, I thought.

The performance was in the hall adjoining the castle. Local choral singers made up the choir. In the grounds, boys were camping, students from Gordonstoun. Among them was Prince Charles, then a boy of around fifteen.

We had a bedroom smelling strongly of mothballs. The big baronial bed was as hard as a rock. Was that why the Scots are so hardy? Kitchens miles away from the dining areas, many stairs to climb, servants discreetly somewhere—there had to be many in such a great place.

Lady Aberdeen wrote to apologise for the mothballs!

I can describe the performance: very good. After all, Richard and Janet and John were singing!

It was after the performance that I remember best. Lord and Lady Aberdeen put on a reception in their castle. Local lairds gathered in dress kilts, lace and velvet. In my romantic mind, it could have been a gathering of Cavaliers and bonny Prince Charlie. Huge fires in every room. And a memorable bit of recall. I had several conversations with our own bonny Prince Charlie... We got on very well. He took a shine to me (although didn't remember me when we dined in Windsor... well, why would he?) He offered to take breakfast up to Mr and Mrs Lewis.

Lady Aberdeen disapproved. Would have been nice for my memoirs though!

You will now be aware that I often see the humorous side of things. It is an obligatory asset in our funny world of make believe. And I must not forget that this is the story of a man who raised himself up to dine with kings.

By now, Richard Lewis was established in the world of top music, in particular, America.

There was not a conductor or producer he had not worked with. His favourites? Some. Not all. Beecham, Sargent, Barbirolli, Boult, Ormandy, Szell, Markevitch, Pritchard, Menuhin, Gui, Bernstein, Davies 1 and 2, Britten, Walter, Dorati, Giulini, Haitink and Solti. As I write, we know their names by the surname only. Fame indeed!

So, which did he admire most? Or to put it another way, which did he not like? Possibly Beecham: very autocratic, difficult, didn't like women. His witticisms were famous. To many, these witticisms are better known than his work as a conductor. He had a wry sense of humour such as when in a concert performance of *Idomeneo* conducted by him, he subjected Richard in rehearsal to what could have been a humiliating experience. Fortunately, our tenor had a fairly thick hide.

What did Beecham do? When Richard came to the cadenza in the big aria, *Fuor Del Mar*, Beecham listened, made him sing it twice, then said, "Now write it down for me." This was in front of the orchestra and chorus!

Sir Malcolm Sargent: beloved of singers. He and Richard forged a strong relationship. Sargent would always ask for him first during the season. Always immaculate, loved the high life, the aristocracy. Had a nick name 'Flash Harry' from his early days when he rushed about and conducted everything at great speed as well as his love of the upper echelons of society.

Loyal to his favoured singers. A Divorcé. He lived in a block of flats overlooking the Albert Hall. Had a parrot, a very noisy one. If you were lucky enough to be invited to see him, a glass of sherry was always offered. A good conductor? Many people were not sure. Too much the showman for British taste maybe? Or at least the critic's taste!

Eugene Ormandy went to hear him in the Albert Hall.

"I had never heard the slow movement of the *Beethoven Symphony* conducted better."

Giulini came high up on the list. Working with this gentle, quiet-spoken Italian was very satisfying. In one particular work in the Festival Hall (I think it was the Mozart *Requiem*), as it was televised, Giulini asked the soloists to sing it without scores. The result was magnificent.

Igor Markevitch stood out. Not so well known but a major conductor in his day. Small, quixotic, intense. He had been one of the Diaghilev group in Paris. I gathered from his conversation that the Ballets Russes was a hot bed of homosexuality. Not something that Stravinsky dwelt upon in his Los Angeles garden, and not something I would ask.

John Pritchard was a conductor certainly high up in the list. He and Richard had had a long musical association He was a homosexual when it was illegal. Everyone knew. He was a very kind generous man, a fine conductor, especially for Mozart, Music Director at Glyndebourne for a long time. He handled singers very tactfully, necessary in the world of prima donnas, particularly Joan Sutherland. In a *Don Giovanni* rehearsal, Joan went into a long cadenza, written by Richard Bonynge (her husband) and not Mozart. Pritchard managed to get her to drop it with elegant grace and tact.

Glyndebourne do not like prima donnas. If you sang there you had to, as one stage manager said, "Leave your ego outside the door when you get here and pick it up again when you leave." I think I can safely say, with rare exception, that singers, being on the whole a normal modest people, would not find that strange. Maybe one or two arrive with a preconception. I remember one baritone (who shall be nameless) who was sacked quite early!

John Pritchard and Richard went a long way back to their early careers as young men. He came from the same part of the world. For over forty years, they worked together. I got to know Pritchard when I was in Wexford. He was conducting Rossini's *Gazza* Ladra. He was very lonely. I was invited up to his hotel room where we talked long into the night. The life of a top musician can be isolating. Travelling the world alone, one bedroom after another, never time to see where you are, off the next day somewhere else. In spite of his success and renown, a rather sad man.

Wexford is an amazing opera festival. Performances take place in an ancient theatre next door to a pub. Curtain up, approximate. I went with a group of singers from

Glyndebourne. After one performance, I was invited to have a drink in the pub next door, with some friends.

The room was up a steep set of stairs. Full of smoke (the cigarette ban had not yet arrived). Everyone well ahead of us The Irish are very good at enjoying a drink. We were regaled with pints of Guinness, until a little gnome-like man was lifted up onto a table, and looked about to sing. Before doing so, he removed his teeth, hung them on a hook and proceeded to render a folk song sung in Gaelic.

There were two Davis's, one with an e and one without:

Colin Davis and Andrew Davies.

One day, when Richard had decided to do a bit of conducting, he met up with Colin at Covent Garden.

"Colin, I'm thinking of doing a bit of conducting."

"Oh God, not another singer trying to conduct," he exploded.

Singers to conduct. Why not? If the 1st trumpet can stand up or the 2nd violin, why not a singer? A singer is just as capable as an instrumentalist? Mind you, not all, but generally.

He Did Conduct

Richard was invited by the conductor of the Ditchling Choral Society, a major Sussex choir led by an amazing woman. Janet Canetty-Clarke.

"Would he conduct *The Dream of Gerontius*?"

Having sung it for so long, he must have known every note. But he had not conducted it before.

I asked the leader of the orchestra what he thought.

"A natural," he told me.

The soloists were Anthony Rolfe Johnson and I. During the rehearsal, I noticed Anthony looking a bit pale.

"Are you OK?"

"I'm fine, but he's conducting," pointing at Richard. "Who wouldn't be nervous."

Anthony had studied with Richard some years ago.

Talking about singers conducting, I once got into an argument through the *Daily Telegraph* letters with a musician called Gerald Moore no less! (Probably one of the most famous accompanists in the world.)

Robert Tear had taken up the baton. He was a superb musician. Gerald Moore had written to the *Telegraph* to say that he did not agree with singers conducting, "As I have never come across a singer who could count," was his comment. That really annoyed me, so I fired off a letter refuting what Moore had said. They printed it. Gerald Moore then answered it, disagreeing with me.

I wanted to send another. Richard thought it best to leave it. Looking back, I'm sorry. I would have liked to go on, might have been interesting.

Andrew Davies came into Richard's life when Richard's career was nearly over, and Andrew's career was at the early period. He asked Richard to sing *Dream of Gerontius* with him in Liverpool. It was, I believe, his first. For Richard, a poignant place to sing. Why? Because that was where his very first *Gerontius* took place with Sir Malcolm Sargent.

We went up to Liverpool.

Richard was nervous. I had never seen him so nervous.

Why? Well, he was over sixty. And it's a hard sing at any age. Would he still be able to do it? But miracles can happen. That evening, he sang as a young man again. The voice had done something that night. That wayward instrument had turned back the years. I doubt there were many dry eyes in the audience. Just for a while, his youthful voice had returned.

"I can still do it," he told me. I was there. I saw. I heard it.

And Andrew Davies? He said he would never forget it.

I wish I could say the same about Richard's last *Dream of Gerontius* with Bernard Haitink. The Dutch conductor had always wanted to put it on with Richard. And Richard had always wanted to sing it with Haitink. But I must be honest. That was one he should have missed. Against all advice, he decided to do it.

Why against all advice? He was in his mid-sixties. He had just had a second hip replacement. He was out of practice. I tried everything to dissuade him. But he was not a Taurus for nothing. I then suggested that he announced that it would be his swan song, that he was retiring.

"After all, Geraint Evans retired several times."

Critics are always kind if it's a swan song!!

That didn't work. He went ahead. My worst fears were realised. It wasn't terrible. But it was not how he should have been remembered.

Ask any singer. When is the best time to retire? So easy to say when you are still doing it well, but the time comes for everyone.

For Richard, the romantic roles were no more. Maybe character roles would be a good idea. I don't think that appealed to him either. In other words, he was in denial.

One morning, a call came from Raymond Leppard, the conductor at Glyndebourne:

"Would Richard be interested in a role in Monteverdi's *The Return of Ulysses*?"

Of course, he would. Maybe a major part for him.

"Come and have a look at the score, Richard"

So that evening, we went to Leppard's house. After some chat, he handed the score to Richard.

"It's the part of Eumete, the shepherd."

Richard looked through it.

"I only have two scenes, Raymond."

"Important scenes though."

"No, sorry, I'm not ready yet to be assigned to small roles."

We left. I guessed it was up to me to persuade him. For I felt sure that if Raymond thought it was something good for Richard, he should give it serious thought.

I had a bright idea, No idea where it came from.

"Do you remember a film about Friese Greene and the first television images?" It was a 1951 film, The Magic Box, Laurence Olivier played the policeman.

"Yes, I do."

"Can you remember who the main actor was playing Baird?"

"No, I can't."

"Can you remember the small part, the policeman who came up to see the images?"

"Yes, I can. Lawrence Olivier."

"Well, there you are, a small role, but you remember him."

How clever was I! He accepted the next day. His role of Eumete was a great success.

Frederica von Stade and Richard Lewis (Eumete) in Ulysses by
Monteverdi at Glyndebourne

Not a long role, a character role. Many fine singers are
character singers. It's what they do.

Comprimario it's called. Was this then the start of a new
career as a Comprimario? It would have been nice to think so,
but I'm afraid, time caught up with him.

So again, when to retire? That is the question. And I have
a story to indicate how difficult it is and, sometimes, how
tragic. Retirement for the businessman or bank manager,
leaving with a gold watch as a thank you for long service is
different. For singing is a vocation. It's what we would do
even if not paid. The fact that it's paid well is a bonus.

Another Tenor

We were in San Francisco. A supporter had invited us to lunch. When we got there, at the far end of the room sat an old man. The host told us it was Richard Crooks, who had been a very famous pre-war tenor.

Richard went down to see him. After introducing himself, Crooks began to weep.

There in front of us was why it's so difficult.

Richard held his hand, and they talked. Meeting up later, we heard so many stories.

Crooks told us a story about an opera he had sung. Taking over from a resident tenor who was ill, and who was a friend. After he had performed, he went back to his dressing room. The resident tenor was in the toilet.

"As I got to the dressing room door, a voice called, 'Well, I could sing that better sitting on the toilet.'"

A group of tenors. A phalanx of tenors. How can you describe them? They of the broad chests and short necks, of confidence born because they always get the girl, they of the top notes, of Pavarotti, Carreras, Domingo, friends but competitors. Who can get the highest notes or hold a note the longest!

Richard Lewis was not this sort. Yes, he had a broad chest and a short neck, but he was a different kind. His voice was not a strident Italian one. It was an English one. Mellifluous, easy in production, moving. But…

You can sing too long.

"I will never do that," said Richard. "I will know when it's time to give up."

He didn't, of course, but he believed it when he said it! It is not easy to give up the applause, the exciting engagements, telegrams arriving, the work, the involvement, the people, above all. And when it comes, how quickly it ends. How soon you are the older statesman.

How do you fill that gap?

If you are clever, you have a hobby. Did Richard? A few. Played golf, took up miniature trains. But he missed it. Those wonderful people in your life, where do they go? Does it happen to them too?

Teaching

Near the end of Richard's career, he was asked to teach in the Curtis Institute in Philadelphia. He had outstanding pupils and enjoyed passing on his knowledge and was still very much out there performing. For one concert in New York, he hired a car and took his students to the Lincoln Centre to hear him. He felt it was important that they saw what he was teaching put into action.

We were talking about conductors. And who was favourite? Georg Solti.

A Dynamo on two legs. What energy this Hungarian conductor had. He was music director at Covent Garden. In his time there, he not only gave British singers a prominent place in the company, but built Covent Garden to be world class.

Singing with him was like being with a hurricane. But he did not suffer fools or accept bad preparation. If you gave him your best, he was a gentle man.

I had the good fortune to sing with him in America. On the night of the performance, I found myself in the lift taking us to platform level.

"Is there anything you would like," he asked in that attractive, middle-European accent.

"Well, there is a moment at the end of the last act where there is so much going on, it is difficult to hear a cue."

He asked me to show him. We left the lift. That was it. He would not remember.

When the moment came, he not only remembered, but turned to me and gave me an extra-strong cue.

Memory plays tricks sometimes. Particular performances stand out. Either it went well or something funny happened or a disaster.

One comes to mind:

A *Salome* in San Francisco.

The producer: Paul Hager, a German. Richard was Herod, George London, John, and Salome was sung by the German soprano Anja Silja.

The cast had been rehearsing for nearly two weeks, Silja not due to arrive until two days before the opening. One morning, as the cast ran through scenes, Silja made an appearance. She sat watching for a while, then announced that she did not do it this way, wanting changes.

The producer told me he timed it to see how long it would take Richard to react.

"Miss Silja, we have been rehearsing for some weeks. It is too late to start changing things."

He walked out.

He and Silja did not exchange a word throughout the performances. And when Herod, right at the end of the opera sings *Kill that woman*, it was sung with some authority!

Richard Lewis as Herod with Anja Silja as Salome in Salome by Richard Strauss

Geraint Evans was, like Richard, a regular artist with San Francisco Opera. He and Richard had both been fellow soldiers in the war. Both started together and climbed the ladder together.

They appeared together in many productions: *Zauberflöte* and *Don Giovanni* at Glyndebourne, *Zauberflöte* and *Don*

Giovanni at Covent Garden. Together many years in San Francisco. In particular, *Wozzeck* by Alban Berg.

Geraint sang Wozzeck. Richard, the Captain. Marilyn Horne, Marie. Geraint was incredibly moving as Wozzeck. He could also get up to his tricks. In the scene where he is shaving the captain, after a few performances, things begin to loosen up, and he tried to get Richard to 'corpse'.

In the shaving scene, Wozzeck shows the captain a picture. I don't know what the picture was, but it nearly finished Richard! He wouldn't tell me. I took a good guess.

Geraint Evans and Richard Lewis in San Franciso

The two lovers in Mozart's Cosi Fan Tutte in San Francisco Opera

San Francisco

For most singers an invitation to sing with San Francisco Opera is much coveted.

Not only is it a lovely building, efficiently run, but you have the glorious Californian countryside to explore, and of course the city is a fascinating and diverse place to live in with its high hills, and down town roads a perilous journey.

Very few singers turn down the opportunity to perform there.

After rehearsals the singers would go and dine in some of the countless restaurants, from Chinese to British, Indian and European. It has an amazing China Town, and eating there is an adventure. I have had more wonderful meals in America than any other place in the world.

And here I have heard many people, who have never been to America, say it only has hamburgers and fast food!

Quite the opposite.
And the singers. From every part of the world.

The Intendant was Kurt Adler. A rather forbidding looking man who travelled the world seeking great singers for his opera house.

The Americans produce so many wonderful artists in every voice. Why I don't know. Possible because of the way they speak, Rather nasal and resonant. In particular, female voices, and specifically black singers. Two of my most favourite are Leontyne Price and Shirley Verrett. Leontyne is a glorious soprano with a voice of dark velvet. She was the first African American singer to achieve an international reputation in opera.

To show how things have changed since then (The sixties and seventies,) she had to paint her face white to sing in the operatic repertoire, which would be unthinkable today.

Shirley was a mezzo soprano. Tall, statuesque, brimming with intelligence and glamour. We got to know her very well during the season. One evening we were invited to dinner in her San Francisco apartment. As we walked up the stairs Shirley came out to greet us, wearing a deep red velvet dress. With her lovely dark skin and vibrancy, she presented a wonderful picture of beauty and elegance. She was married to a Spaniard. "He is much more passionate about the racial thing" she told me "He goes on marches."

And of course, it was not easy for black artists, whoever they were, whether jazz musicians or classical singers.

Shirley told me how she would have an ovation at the Metropolitan Opera in New York, and be refused entrance to any restaurant. This was long before our present "Black Lives Matter," and brings home to one how terrible that was.

Memories of making music in that amazing city have stayed with me ever since. We rented a small flat in Sausalito, over the Golden Gate Bridge. From our kitchen you could see the city with its sky scrapers hanging above the morning mist which rolled in. A weird and wonderful sight.

In all the great cities I have seen, San Francisco is my first choice.

The life of a singer is one of constant travel. While it might look exciting on paper, the reality can often be the opposite. Hours of travel in air-conditioned planes. Holed up in hotels (The voice has to be protected) Hours of rehearsal. Standing, waiting.

Yes, at the end of it. The performance. That's when the best bit starts. Fine costumes. Great conductors (mostly),

Friends and colleagues all sharing the same buzz of performing.

We toured for eight months of the year. Suitcases filled with the same old clothes. I was the suitcase organiser, as Richard wanted to take far too much stuff with him. But I did get fed up with such a long time away with no home life. And let me tell you that clothes become too familiar. How many times did I hang a dress over the steam from the bath, trying get creases out (There were no hotel services in those days)

Bermuda

One year (1966) we went to Bermuda to give a concert. A working holiday really. Balmy climes. Tropical heat. Cold and wet England seemed a long way off.

One evening, after dinner with the governor, Richard casually mentioned.

"How would you like to live here?"

"Well, why not"

So, we sold our Sussex home, found a house on a hill (Harrington Sound) and started a new life. From the island we could fly over to the States. And our life became less hectic, plus we were able to have a baby, who is now a grown man.

It is an island of white roofed houses. Walls coloured pink, pale blue. or yellow. There are no water pipes or drainage on the island. Water is provided by the rain falling from the roofs into a large water container that stretched the length the houses, so as there are copious amounts of rain all year, a water supply was never a problem.

One year, when back in the UK, we rented our house to an American family. On our return we found we had very little water in our tank, so had to buy some, costing a vast amount. The next day, it rained! We would see our money running down the hill as it overflowed!

We lived on the island for six years, and great years they were.

Island life is an odd one. A large proportion of the residents are British and American It is a real polyglot of the two nations. Many of the British set had a scheme to dodge tax. You buy a grave in preparation to die there one day, and the tax man leaves you alone.

We have no grave prepared for us there!

Being in the celebrity class (I was told) we were welcomed by the artistic fraternity which is large and active. Made friends with many interesting people. One was Geoffrey Tankard. A Royal Academy piano teacher who had come to live on the Island. Through him we started to give concerts, ending up organising a music festival in the lovely Town Hall.

We took up golf. Learning on one of the most beautiful (and difficult) golf courses in the world. It is in Tuckers Town, the playground of the wealthy. A glorious golf club on the edge of the ocean. Many of the shots stay in the memory.

One tee off was from the top of a cliff. The golfer had to hit a shot over a vast space of ocean to the other side. It was a daunting shot. My coach told me to shut my eyes and pray!

We had six great years there. There Richard could say goodbye to the Manchester fogs and smogs, finding life in the sun, a pleasant respite from performing.

There is a huge population of black residents on the island. Many descendants of slaves.

When we arrived, there was segregation. Which I found difficult. By the time we left six years later that had all gone. Not without many battles verbal and otherwise.

One year there were riots. Black workers marching to get more equality. The marches went by our house. I was alone at that time. I had a new baby. I was quite prepared to go out a window into the bushes above the house. Fortunately, they passed by. But it was pretty scary.

The Island is a strange mixture of British and American influences. The money was in dollars. The way of life was American. But it was a British colony, with a governor. Americans dominated the population. Many of the Bermudian wives were American. Many of the Brits were the old school.

It made a strange cultural mix.

Many years later, after Richard had died, I went back to give a concert with the choral society.

There were two performances. One in George Town (The original town) Standing in the square with the sky above, the orchestra behind me, the audience in front, my voice reverberated round the square. The only thing was that every time I sat down my chair moved back a fraction, until in the end I fell into the first violins.

The final concert was in a field. I wouldn't recommend this to any young singer. I doubt if the audience, having picnics, and generally larking about, heard any of the music. My singing "O Mio Babbino Caro" got lost and disappeared for ever.

I stayed with friends, the Triminghams. Mary Lou and John Trimingham were the younger members of the Trimingham family, who owned a store on front street.

The shops there are wonderfully expensive. Everything is imported of course, so the quality has to be good, plus tourists arrive with money to spend.

Mary Lou and John let me stay with them in Tuckers Town. The best area of the Island, where the very rich live. However, it doesn't matter how much you have in the bank when it comes to natural things. One night I was asleep, when I was woken by a sort of shuffling sound. Putting on the light I saw an army of cockroaches marching towards me. Very big, very nasty looking. Needless to say I disappeared quickly, and John rang the pest control. I did not sleep in that room again.

One pleasant occasion was when a film was put on in the golf club in the gardens, where the stars were our companions. Can one forget those balmy evenings, with the moon overheard?

So, life was pleasant. I had a nanny. Well for a while. Mrs Green. An efficient little woman, who looked after our son when we were away. She told me how one night there was an earthquake during the night.

When I asked her what she did, she just said, "Took Nigel into my bed, and we stayed there until the morning. My son told me what fun it had been!"

Then I thought how nice it would be if Mrs Green stayed on when we returned, so we could play golf. What I hadn't anticipated was that I was not allowed to do anything. Not bath Nigel; Or put him to bed. Or play or read to him. After two days I'd had enough. Mrs Green had to go. But she was a good nanny.

We had a Volkswagen Estate all the time we were there. A great little car. When we were to leave, I tried to sell it to a dealer.

"Sorry, we don't buy second hand cars"

"Well, what do you do to one?" I asked.

"Take it out to sea and dump it."

That whole idea appalled me. So, we decided to take it to England.

For £45. It arrived back. We picked it up. And drove it for another ten years. Then sold it.

But to show what a durable little car it was, one day, after selling it, it passed me on the road with its new owners.

I didn't see it wave, but I thought I saw it grinning.

Thank goodness the public don't know or see things that happen. Take a Zauberflöte at Covent Garden. Conducted by Klemperer. Geraint Evans, Papageno, and Richard, Tamino.

In the opera, the two singers have some dialogue. Trumpets sound. The two men came in (in rehearsal) and as they began speaking, Klemperer brought the trumpets in too soon, drowning the voices.

"Maestro, can you wait until we finish the dialogue," called Richard.

They tried again. The same thing happened. Then a third time... in frustration, Richard threw his flute at the backdrop curtain, "Dr Klemperer, you must wait."

Finally, they got it right. An orchestra player told Richard, "Dr Klemperer said, 'Well, that was a tussle.'"

However, he had taken note. For as Richard sang *Dies Bildnis* the big aria, on the first night, Klemperer took out a large hankie and blew his nose loudly.

Singers are divided up into those who sing opera and those who don't.

Singers who sing only recital and oratorio, singers who sing only opera. And those who do both. Richard was the latter. He liked to move from one style to another.

"Keeps my voice agile."

Let me explain why.

A singer who is an accomplished lieder (song) singer can be at a disadvantage when they sing opera. I always thought that Fischer-Dieskau was in that category. A most wonderful lieder singer, a superb oratorio performer. As an opera singer, disappointing, too cerebral.

Lieder singing (or song singing), which has a character that has a similar character in an opera is interpreted differently. *Mignon* is a good example. Often used by composers, as in say Schubert's Lieds (*Lied der Mignon*) is quite different to Gounod's *Mignon* in *Goethe's Faust (Margarita)*.

The pure song singer has an inner life, a cerebral art form. The opera singer's is outgoing, extrovert. His inner world is communicating through acting with voice and body, the song recitalist through inner intellectual thought.

So what sort was our tenor?

He was an introvert man, an extrovert on stage. He could do both. At his happiest singing and acting. That cloistered untouchable world.

A funny old make-believe one!

One last story: a human one, a wonderful one, a funny one—all of those.

One day, we decided to go and visit Norman Allin, Richard's old teacher. We knew he was in a retirement home for musicians and singers somewhere in Hampshire.

We drove down and found this attractive place set in beautiful countryside. Going in, we were startled to find so many people we had known were residents. Out of the lounge

144

came face after face of famous singers and players so pleased to see an old colleague.

It was surreal, even made us feel guilty to be still out there full of vigour. On the other hand, they were among their own kind, remembering how it was, recalling the buzz of performance.

"Can we see Norman?"

"He may not be up yet. Let's go and see."

The attendant took us up to Norman's room. He knocked on the door. A deep bass voice said, "Come in."

We opened the door. Norman Allin was sitting on his bed with his back to us. Richard did something that still gives me goose pimples.

He began singing *Dalla Sua Pace* from *Don Giovanni*.

Norman's back straightened, "Richard!"

For two hours, I sat listening to these two men reminiscing. What a long life they had to remember. How much Richard had to thank this wonderful singer for.

We had a cup of tea. Then saw that Norman was getting tired.

"We must go Norman," Richard said.

"Thank you for coming," said this great person, "and what a fine son you have," shaking hands with me. His sight was so bad that he thought I was a boy! I didn't mind!

That visit was so poignant, not just because we saw Norman. Sad to see that it all comes to an end, that so many great musicians have a life that only has memories after the last note is sounded.

On the other hand, they had had it, done it, known the joys of making music.

Seeing so many artists of long ago, did they remember what it was like to step out to sing or play? Live again their triumphs.

And if you want to know a bit more about the subject of this book, if you have read the first chapters, you can guess that his beginnings never really left him. Those Manchester pea soup fogs never went away. Always in his heart, he dreaded that all that he had done and achieved would disappear into the mist. How our past directs our future. Losing his Manchester accent, changing his name, mixing with people who had they known him then might have turned away. His roots were Welsh. But he rejected his forebears. He acquired a new skin, a new name. No longer Thomas Thomas, he became Richard Lewis.

He wanted what we all want. Success. Fame. Money. But in his heart, he hankered for something else. That was why he loved America. There he was who he was without any background. He was only what they could see and hear. Not judged by where he came from.

He felt safe there.

A 70th Birthday

No one wants to reach seventy, especially a singer, when it's all over and old age the only thing to wait for. So how to make it special?

I went to see Geoffrey Gilbertson, the stage manager at Glyndebourne.

"Let's have a surprise party in the restaurant."

So planning began. Colleagues, past and present, were invited. Some could come, some not. Pavarotti sent a note, "To my special colleague and my inspiration."

I had to hide what was going on, getting the post, making sure he didn't suspect anything. He said afterwards he had wondered what I was up to!

The day May 10th arrived. Everything had been set up. Our two boys kept the guests happy. Sir Georg Solti and his wife Valerie were among the waiting crowd.

George and Mary Christie had invited us for a drink. In the great drawing room, we sat and chatted, until Mary gave me a wink, and we both went to the bathroom.

"Let's get him up to the restaurant on the pretext of seeing some new photos."

We went down again.

"Come on, Richard, leave the drink, and let's go and see these photos," Mary said.

Walking up the slope to the restaurant, it was very quiet. The boys had done a good job.

Elizabeth Muir-Lewis (the author) with her son Nigel (left) and her stepson Michael

We went in; so many friends and colleagues. He was so surprised, I thought he might have a stroke… Solti came and embraced him.

It was a night to remember: terrific food, champagne, a lovely way to celebrate. Glyndebourne made it all happen. This man was a special singer who had stayed through thick and thin to be able to sing there. You could say it was his beginning and his end. During the next few weeks, I waited for the bill to arrive. Eventually, I rang Geoffrey.

"Have you forgotten?"

"It's on the house, Elizabeth." Now how about that!

After he died, I found a sponsor to fund a trust to remember him. Dr Jean Shanks, a distinguished pathologist gave us a huge amount of money when she died.

Over the years, we have funded various projects: Cardiff Singer of the World, Glyndebourne's John Christie Award in conjunction with the Worshipful Company of Musicians.

But none seemed to be right... either they were too big (Glyndebourne, Cardiff) or the money was assisting singers already on their way. We needed to find the right level that would help singers needing money at that important time in their development.

We decided to go to the Royal Academy of Music, the place where Richard had studied for a short time after the war, and where we would help young singers at that vulnerable time before setting out into the profession.

With this fund of over a million pounds, we sponsor one of Britain's biggest singing awards.

It is now over twenty years. In that time, a long lines of wonderful young singers have benefitted from this fund.

To name a few:

Emma Bell, Lucy Crowe, Alan Clayton, Clara Mouritz, David Butt Philip, Roberto Ortiz, Rodney Clarke, Sarah Tynan, among many others. Some international, all working. The 2021 winner was Patrick Keefe

There is also the Webb Award for the best accompanist, donated by a great friend, Brenda Webb

This has also discovered some superb players.

As a last comment. To be in this wonderful profession called music making, those who practice the great art are the lucky ones in the world. It is a hard world of stress and strain. But I hope I have given some idea of the joy and ecstasy of our world... Music and song.

THE END

Elizabeth, the Author

Richard Lewis Discography

Compiled by Brian Godfrey

INDEX OF WORKS

BACH, Johann Sebastian
Cantata No.80
Cantata No.104
Easter Oratorio, BWV249
Magnificat in D, BWV243
St. John Passion, BWV245

BARTÓK, Béla
Cantata profana *[English]*

BEETHOVEN, Ludwig van
Christus am Ölberge, Op.85
Mass in C, Op.86
Missa Solemnis in D, Op.123
Symphony No.9 in D minor, Op.125

BERLIOZ, Hector
Benvenuto Cellini (cpte)
Grande Messe des Morts, Op.5

BIZET, Georges
Le jolie fille de Perth (cpte) *[English]*
Les pêcheurs de perles – Je crois entendre encore

BLISS, Sir Arthur
The Beatitudes

BOUGHTON, Rutland
The Immortal Hour – The Faery song

BRAHMS, Johannes
Liebeslieder Walzer, Op.52
Neue Liebeslieder Walzer, Op.65

BRITTEN, Benjamin
Spring Symphony, Op.44

BRUCKNER, Anton
Te Deum

BUSONI, Ferruccio
Doktor Faust (cpte)

CAVALLI, Francesco
Egisto – Musici della selva

COLERIDGE TAYLOR, Samuel
Hiawatha's Wedding Feast, Op.30 No.1

CORNELIUS, Peter
Auftrag

DOWLAND, John

Come away, come sweet love, if you change
Flow not so fast, ye fountains A shepherd in the shade
Sorrow stay
Weep you no more, sad fountains
Whoever thinks or hopes of love for love

ELGAR, Sir Edward

The Dream of Gerontius, Op.38

HANDEL, George Frederic

Acis and Galatea (cpte)
Acis and Galatea – Would you gain Alexander's Feast – War,
he sung35 Giulio Cesare – V'adoro pupille
Israel in Egypt
Israel in Egypt (ed. Sargent)
Jephtha – For ever blessed
Jephtha – Waft her, angels
Jephtha – While Kedron's brook
Judas Maccabaeus – How vain is man, Judas Maccabaeus –
Sound and alarm Messiah
Messiah – excs
Samson – Total eclipse
Semele – Where'er you walk
Serse – Ombra mai fù
Serse – Quelle che tutta

LISZT, Franz

Wie singt die Lerche schön, S312

LULLY, Jean-Baptiste
Miserere

MAHLER, Gustav
Das Lied von der Erde

MASSENET, Jules
Manon – En fermant les yeux

MENDELSSOHN, Felix
Elijah (cpte)
Elijah – excs

MONTEVERDI, Claudio
L'incoronazione di Poppea (abridged) Orfeo – Qual onor di
te fia degno
Il ritorno d'Ulisse in patria (cpte) Vespers, 1610

MOZART, Wolfgang
Così fan tutte (cpte)
Così fan tutte – excs
Don Giovanni (cpte)
Die Entführung – Ach! Belmonte Idomeneo (cpte)
Idomeneo – excs
Mass in C minor, K427
Requiem in D minor, K626
Der Schauspieldirektor (cpte) *[English]*
Die Zauberflöte (cpte)

MUNRO, George
My lovely Celia

PUCCINI, Giacomo
La bohème – Si sento meglio?
Madama Butterfly: Viene la sera
Manon Lescaut – Tu, tu amore
Tosca: E lucevan le stelle – O dolci mani

PURCELL, Henry
Fairest isle, Z628
In the black, dismal dungeon, Z190
Music for a while, Z583
Sleep, Adam, sleep, Z195
Welcome song – What, what shall be done?, Z341

SCHÖNBERG, Arnold
Gurre-Lieder

STAINER, Sir John
The Crucifixion

STRAUSS, Johann II
Die Fledermaus – excs *[English]*

STRAUSS, Richard
Elektra (cpte)
Salome (cpte)

STRAVINSKY, Igor
Persephone

SULLIVAN, Sir Arthur
The Gondoliers (cpte)

HMS Pinafore (cpte)
The Mikado (cpte)
The Pirates of Penzance (cpte)
Ruddigore (cpte)
Trial by Jury (cpte)
The Yeomen of the Guard (cpte)

TIPPETT, Sir Michael
A Child of our Time
The Midsummer Marriage (cpte)
King Priam – O rich soiled land

TRADITIONAL
All through the night
Bingo
The briery bush
Buy broom buzzems
David of the White Rock
The Eriskay Love-lilt
Fine flow'rs in the valley
The foggy, foggy dew
The Helston furry dance
I will give my love an apple
King Arthur's servants Leezie Lindsay
The Maypole Song
My brown-haired maid O love it is a killing thing O Waly,
Waly
She moved thro' the Fair The stuttering lovers
There's none to soothe

VAUGHAN WILLIAMS, Ralph Hodie
On Wenlock Edge
Serenade to Music

VERDI, Giuseppe
Requiem Mass

WAGNER, Richard
Der fliegende Holländer (cpte)

WALTON, Sir William
Troilus and Cressida – excs

YOUNG, Anthony
Phillis has such charming graces

List of Composers
And Conductors

Barbirolli, Sir John
Beecham, Sir Thomas
Bernard, Anthony
Bernstein, Leonard
Bliss, Sir Arthur
Böhm, Karl
Boult, Sir Adrian
Busch, Fritz
Danon, Oskar
Davis, Colin
Dorati, Antál
Giulini, Carlo Maria
Goehr, Walter
Goldsbrough, Arnold
Guest, George
Gui, Vittorio
Horenstein, Jascha
Jones, Geraint
Klemperer, Otto
Krips, Josef
Leibowitz, René

Leinsdorf, Erich

Leppard, Raymond

Lewis, Anthony

Maazel, Lorin

Mackerras, Sir Charles

Ormandy, Eugene

Previn, André

Pritchard, John

Reiner, Fritz

Sargent, Sir Malcolm

Savill, Patrick

Shaw, Robert

Solti, Georg

Somary, Johannes

Stravinsky, Igor

Süsskind, Walter

Szell, Georg

Vandernoot, André

Vaughan Williams, Ralph

Walter, Bruno

Walton, Sir William

Westrup, Jack

Willcocks, David

Review Of

"When the Last Note Sounds"
By Elizabeth Muir-Lewis

It is good to be reminded of the illustrious career of one of Britain's finest tenors of the 20 th century. Richard Lewis performed a prodigious range of music encompassing works by Purcell and Tippett, Bach and Stravinsky - and much else in between.

But Elizabeth Muir Lewis's biographical memoir reveals other aspects of this great artist – the husband, the father and the colleague. We read of his relationships with other singers and conductors – sometimes friendly, at other times less so – and his worldwide travels to sing at some of the world's most prestigious venues.

Only a partner who knew him as well as Elizabeth could tell his story in such a fascinating and entertaining way.

Paul Campion
Well known author on Music

When the Last Note Sounds
By Elizabeth Muir-Lewis.

Written by the second wife of the great tenor Richard Lewis (1914-90), this volume is less a formal biography than a memoir by the person closest to him, a fellow singer who shared his life from the early 1960s onwards.

Her understanding of the voice and the world of performance are assets in recounting Lewis's career, one of the most successful of his time, and fully international: he enjoyed particular success in America and especially San Francisco. Of Welsh extraction, Lewis was born with the repetitive name of Thomas Thomas in Manchester in 1914 (an early poster names the fine boy soprano as 'Tom Thomas, the wonderful boy singer from Ardwick, Manchester'). It was his teacher Norman Allin who insisted on a change of name for professional purposes: Richard came from the admired Tauber; Lewis was his mother's maiden name.

Just as Lewis was on the point of launching his career, World War II got in the way; but while subsequently a post-war mature student at the Royal Academy of Music, the extraordinary quality of his voice and his impeccable musicianship soon saw him in demand with the English Opera

Group, at Glyndebourne (hundreds of performances between 1947 and 1979, with Mozart to the fore) and the Royal Opera House (an almost identical period). Although the general shape of the book is chronological, the informality of approach allows Muir-Lewis to home in on certain works and professional relationships that were highlights of a career whose sheer range would be hard to match: the pre-eminent Gerontius of his generation (he later conducted the work), Lewis sang in the premieres of Walton's Troilus and Cressida and Tippett's The Midsummer Marriage and King Priam, the first UK performance of The Rake's Progress— which became a regular assignment (Stravinsky also wrote his Canticum Sacrum for him)—and the first UK staging of Schoenberg's Moses und Aron, an opera he also sang in Paris and in concert in the USA. In addition, there were premieres by Arwell Hughes, Giselher Klebe and Luigi Nono. He made several recordings of Das Lied von der Erde, and his substantial discography also includes a clutch of the Gilbert & Sullivan operas under Malcolm Sargent. There would still be room for a more detailed account of this major career. Muir-Lewis's volume is light but evocative, much of her content anecdotal, but certainly first-hand.

Review by George Hall.